Beginning Application Lifecycle Management

Joachim Rossberg

Apress®

Publisher: Heinz Weinheimer
Acquisitions Editor: Gwenan Spearing
Developmental Editor: Douglas Pundick
Technical Reviewer: Jakob Ehn and Mathias Olausson
Editorial Board: Steve Anglin, Mark Beckner, Ewan Buckingham, Gary Cornell, Louise Corrigan,
    James DeWolf, Jonathan Gennick, Robert Hutchinson, Michelle Lowman, James Markham, Matthew Moodie,
    Jeff Olson, Jeffrey Pepper, Douglas Pundick, Ben Renow-Clarke, Dominic Shakeshaft, Gwenan Spearing,
    Matt Wade, Steve Weiss
Coordinating Editor: Rita Fernando
Copy Editor: Tiffany Taylor
Compositor: SPi Global
Indexer: SPi Global
Cover Designer: Anna Ishchenko

Distributed to the book trade worldwide by Springer Science+Business Media New York, 233 Spring Street, 6th Floor, New York, NY 10013. Phone 1-800-SPRINGER, fax (201) 348-4505, e-mail orders-ny@springer-sbm.com, or visit www.springeronline.com. Apress Media, LLC is a California LLC and the sole member (owner) is Springer Science + Business Media Finance Inc (SSBM Finance Inc). SSBM Finance Inc is a Delaware corporation.

For information on translations, please e-mail rights@apress.com, or visit www.apress.com.

Apress and friends of ED books may be purchased in bulk for academic, corporate, or promotional use. eBook versions and licenses are also available for most titles. For more information, reference our Special Bulk Sales–eBook Licensing web page at www.apress.com/bulk-sales.

Any source code or other supplementary material referenced by the author in this text is available to readers at www.apress.com. For detailed information about how to locate your book's source code, go to www.apress.com/source-code/.

For Eddie and Amelie.

Contents at a Glance

Contents

About the Author

Joachim Rossberg has worked as an IT consultant since 1998. He is primarily a scrum master and project manager but has an extensive history as a system developer/designer. He has demonstrated his technical background with various achievements over the years: MCSD, MCDBA, MCSA, and MCSE. His specialties include agile project management, ALM process, and Team Foundation Server. Joachim is now working for Solidify in Gothenburg, Sweden.

About the Technical Reviewers

Jakob Ehn is currently a Microsoft Visual Studio ALM MVP and also a Visual Studio ALM Ranger. Jakob has 15 years experience in the IT industry, and currently works as a senior consultant at Active Solution. Prior to that he was a solution architect at Inmeta Crayon ASA, specializing in Visual Studio ALM. Jakob is a co-author of the *Team Foundation Server 2012 Starter* book from Packt Publising, and he actively participates in the MSDN forums and contributes to different open source projects, such as the Community TFS Build Extensions and the Community TFS Build Manager. Jakob's blog: http://geekswithblogs.net/Jakob Jakob's Twitter: @JakobEhn.

Mathias Olausson works as the ALM practice lead for Solidify, specializing in software craftsmanship and application lifecycle management. With over 15 years of experience as a software consultant and trainer, he has worked in numerous projects and organizations. Mathias has been a Microsoft Visual Studio ALM MVP for five years and is also active as a Visual Studio ALM. Mathias is a frequent speaker on Visual Studio and Team Foundation Server at conferences and industry events and blogs at http://blogs.msmvps.com/molausson.

Acknowledgments

Thanks to all who helped me through this book. No one mentioned, no one forgotten.

■ ■ ■

CHAPTER 1

Why Application Lifecycle Management Matters

Application Lifecycle Management (ALM) is an area of rapidly growing interest in the development community. ALM is all about how you can manage the entire cycle of building software. With a good ALM process in place, you can develop software faster, more cost effectively, and with greater quality than before. This book shows you what ALM is and why it matters.

Modern organizations depend on software and software systems in many ways. Business processes are often implemented in a digital flow; and without software to support this, even small companies can experience problems. For most companies, the world has changed quickly in the last few years, and they need to adapt constantly.

If you want information these days, it's available at your fingertips all the time. It hasn't always been this way. You might remember the days back when you were a teenager. Music and movies were, and always will be, two of the top interests. For Joachim, this obsession started during my teen years, and he chased rare records by his favorite artists, and hard-to-find horror movies. When he found a rare vinyl pressing of a precious record from the United States, for instance, he was ecstatic—not to mention the emotional turmoil he experienced when he managed to purchase a Japanese edition of the same record. In those days, he wrote snail mail asking for mail-order record catalogs from all over the world, based on ads in magazines such as *Rolling Stone* and *Melody Maker*. After carefully considering what he wanted to purchase, he wrote the purchase order, enclosed crisp bills, and sent a letter with the order inside. Then came the long wait for the package. And believe us, this wait could be long indeed. Nowadays, you can access the Internet, check some sites, and directly purchase what you want using a credit card. The stock available at many sites is huge compared to what it was in Joachim's teens, and you can usually find what you want very quickly. In a few days the package comes, and you can begin using the things you bought.

Responding to Change

These days, communication is different as well. Sites such as Facebook, Twitter, and so on have generated millions of followers not only among early adopters of technology, but from societies as a whole. The numbers of smartphones (iPhones, Android devices, Windows Phones, and more), tablets, and other means of communication have exploded, at least in the parts of the world where the related infrastructure is available.

With the new opportunities that organizations have to do business, much has changed in the world, including the reality for companies. Businesses now have to deal with a global environment, which presents both opportunities and challenges. Commerce has changed and still is changing at a rapid pace. You need to be clear about why you develop business systems and software. For companies, the software-development process has changed as well. Nowadays many organizations have large development teams working on software to support the businesses. Many times these teams are spread globally. This poses many potential problems, such as collaboration issues, source code maintenance, requirements management, and so on. Without processes to support modern software development, business can suffer.

This complex world means organizations encounter new challenges constantly. In order to respond to these changes, ALM becomes increasingly important. Development teams in organizations can use new collaboration tools such as Visual Studio Team Foundation Server from Microsoft, HP Application Lifecycle Management, and similar products from Atlassian and IBM. These tools are ALM platforms that tie together a company's business side with its information technology (IT) side.

ALM is the process an organization uses to care for an application or software system from its conception to its retirement. It's the glue that binds the development processes and defines the efforts necessary to coordinate those processes.

Understanding the Cornerstones of Business

First let's define the term *business*. What do we mean when we talk about this concept? We also need to reach an understanding of what *business software* is, so you don't think of something different when we use that term. When we discuss business in this book, we're talking about not only the commercial part of the company, but all the functions of the company, including human resources, procurement, and so on. This means business software is intended not only for e-commerce, but for all the functions in an enterprise.

Three cornerstones of business system development are important:

- Processes
- Business rules
- Information

These three are dependent on each other. Let's makes an analogy with the human body. If the processes are the muscles of your company and the rules are the brain and the nervous system, you can see information as the spine. None of them could function without the others.

Processes

A company uses different *processes* to support its business. For developers, project managers, software designers, and people with other roles in a development project, it's easy just to focus on the development process. They're often interested in development processes such as the Scrum process or the Extreme Programming (XP) process. Business people mostly focus on the business side, of course, and have no interest in learning about the development process.

A large company needs processes for procurement, sales, manufacturing, and so on—the development process is just one of them. The other processes are necessary for the company to function and survive. Obviously, business processes are valid not only for commercial companies, but for all organizations, including those in the public sector.

SCRUM, XP, AND RUP

If you don't have the full picture of what Scrum, XP, and the Rational Unified Process (RUP) are, we cover them later in this section. For now, suffice it to say that they're development process models you can use to control project development efforts.

Scrum is an iterative and incremental agile software-development method for managing software projects and product or application development (http://en.wikipedia.org/wiki/Scrum_(development)). Although Scrum was intended for management of software-development projects, it can be used in running software maintenance teams or as a program-management approach.

Extreme Programming (XP) is a software-development methodology that is intended to improve software quality and responsiveness to changing customer requirements. As a type of agile software development, it advocates frequent releases in short development cycles (timeboxing), which is intended to improve productivity and introduce checkpoints where new customer requirements can be adopted.

The *Rational Unified Process (RUP)* is an iterative software-development process framework created by the Rational Software Corporation, a division of IBM since 2003. RUP is not a single concrete prescriptive process, but rather an adaptable process framework, intended to be tailored by development organizations and software project teams that select the elements of the process that are appropriate for their needs. RUP is a specific implementation of the Unified Process.

Business Rules

The second cornerstone of business system development is the *business rules* the organization needs in order to function well. Business rules tell you what you can and can't do in the company. For example, a business rule for a retail company might state that no credit check is to be performed on return customers. They also tell you what you *must* do.

 As mentioned earlier, if you compare the processes to the muscles of your body, you can say the rules are equivalent to your brain and nervous system—that is, the things controlling your actions and deeds. Most business rules are relatively stable over time; but as your competitors change, you might need to change your rules as well. When that happens, you need a good process for handling required changes to your software so that it can support changed or added rules.

Information

A third cornerstone of any company is its *information*: that is, information about the company and what is going on within it. This includes all customer information, order information, product catalogs, and so on. Without access to relevant information at the correct time, the business quite simply can't function. Consider this example: it's impossible for a company to sell any of its products if it has no information about which products it has or what price they sell for.

Understanding the Need for Business Software

The reason business software exists is to support the business. Business software should take business needs and requirements and turn them into business value through the use of business software. ALM is one of the processes that can help you deliver this business value. And if IT people do a poor job of building this kind of software or systems because they have a broken ALM process, the business will obviously suffer.

 This is the reason you need to think constantly about why you develop business software and business systems. (No, you don't have to think about it in your free time, even though your manager probably thinks you should.) You don't write software for an enterprise to fulfill your technological wishes alone; you write it to make the business run more smoothly and to create more value (see Figure 1-1). This does not, however, make it less cool or interesting to learn new technology or write smarter code. Fortunately, these are important parts of any software or system.

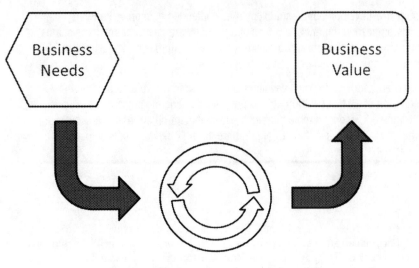

Software Development Lifecycle

Figure 1-1. *The reason you write business software is to turn business needs and opportunities into business value*

Today's Business Environment and the Problems We Face

With the new business opportunities organizations have today, much has changed in terms of the realities we face:

- Companies have to deal with a global environment, which presents both opportunities and challenges. A global way of doing business means competition can come from all sorts of places. Low-cost countries such as China and India can offer many of the same products and services as high-cost countries. This is a challenge for development organizations all over the world. Consulting firms are opening development shops in low-cost countries, and other companies use the services they provide. An organization's internal development department may also see its work move to these countries. So no matter where you work, globalization affects you and your job, and competition is fierce. In order to handle this situation, it's essential to have control over your ALM process. Through this process, you can find support for collaboration between dispersed teams, which can give you the competitive edge you need to face competition from others. You need to automate and fine-tune the ALM process used in your organization so that you can face challenges, keep costs down, and win deals.

- Businesses must become more agile—ready to transform quickly to gain competitive advantages. This obviously affects the way you must architect and write business systems. The ALM process addresses these topics and can help you achieve agility.

- Communication has become increasingly complex. Production of products and services is spread around the world; gone are the days when one industrial plant supplied everything for a company. If software development moves to a country such as India or China, IT needs to handle it somehow. Consider the potential communication problems in a company with offices or manufacturing spread across the globe—not to mention issues with time and cultural differences.

As you can see, business processes can (and do) change rapidly. Hence, the supporting IT systems must also be ready for quick changes. If you don't have systems that allow this, business will suffer. This is one of the main reasons ALM tools such as Microsoft Team Foundation Server (TFS), HP Application Lifecycle Management, and similar products from Atlassian and IBM have emerged. Without an effective development process tied closely to the business side and supported by a set of tools, you can run into problems and risk being left behind by competitors already using such tools. And it isn't only the ALM tools that are important; you need to consider the entire ALM process, including the way you run your development projects.

Project Health Today: Three Criteria for Success

What do we mean when we talk about project health? How can you measure this? With some slight variation, many surveys indicate the same primary criteria for success (or failure, if you're so inclined):

- Project delivered on time

- Project delivered on budget

- Project goals met

Let's discuss these three a bit. Is it reasonable to use these criteria to evaluate project success or failure? We're a bit skeptical and will explain why.

Project Delivered on Time

In traditional project models, a lot of effort is put into time estimates based on the requirements specifications. This way of estimating was (and still is) great for construction of buildings, roads, aircraft, and other traditional engineering efforts. These are the types of projects traditional project-management wisdom comes from.

Such projects are far more static than most software-development projects. The engineering discipline is also rigorous in its requirements-management process, which helps a lot. You don't see as many changes to requirements during the process, and the ones that do occur go through a comprehensive change-request process. Many companies use Capability Maturity Model Integration (CMMI) to improve their process and thus be better at controlling projects. CMMI enables an organization to implement process improvement and show the process's level of maturity.[1]

CMMI can be used to guide process improvement across a project, a division, or an entire organization. The model helps integrate traditionally separate organizational functions, set process improvement goals and priorities, provide guidance for quality processes, and provide a point of reference for appraising current processes.

Based on some experiences at the Swedish Road Administration (SRA), where Joachim has been for seven years, design risks when building a road, for instance, are pretty low; design costs are small, especially compared to building costs; and so on. Here you set the design (or architecture) early in the project based on pretty fixed requirements. From this, you can more easily divide the work into smaller pieces and spread them elegantly across a Gantt chart. This also means you can assign resources based on a fixed schedule. Another benefit is that project management is easier because you can check off completed tasks against the Gantt schema and have better control over when tasks are completed and if there is a delay or lack of resources during the process. On the other hand, if you get an engineering process wrong, lots of money has been wasted; and in the worst case, somebody loses their life because of poor control of the process.

When it comes to more complex building, such as a new tunnel the SRA built in Gothenburg that was opened in 2006, things are a bit different. A tunnel of this magnitude wasn't something the construction companies built every day. This made it harder for the team to estimate the time and money required for the tunnel. In this case, the tunnel's opening date differed from the estimated date only by a couple of months, which must be considered well done because the whole project took more than five years to complete. The reason was that everything from risk management to change requests, and all construction-related tasks, were handled with rigorous processes.

---

[1]Software Engineering Institute, "What Is CMMI?" http://whatis.cmmiinstitute.com/#home.

▓ **Note**   We think one thing that differs greatly between construction processes and software-development processes is that construction workers know that if they make a mistake, somebody might get hurt or die. We in the software-development industry tend not to see that connection clearly, as long as we aren't working with software for hospitals or other such areas. This could be one reason we haven't implemented better processes sooner.

When it comes to IT projects with a lot of development effort, things change. Project uncertainty increases because there are so many ways for things to change unexpectedly. This inherent uncertainty in complex IT projects makes it hard to estimate tasks correctly early on. Things happen along the way that throw off earlier estimates.

Considering this, is it realistic to measure a complex IT project against planned time? To really know how projects are doing, you might want to consider whether this is just one of the measurements you can use.

Project Delivered on Budget

Much of the same reasoning in estimating the time of a project applies to estimating costs, because so much of the cost is tied to the people doing the work. But cost involves other factors as well. You have software costs, office costs, and other costs; but these are often easier to estimate than development costs because they're fixed for the office you use for development. You can put a price tag on a developer, for example, based on that person's total cost (including location costs, training, administrative overhead, and other overhead costs), the cost of leasing a computer, and the cost of software licenses. This can be done in advance, and you then know that one developer costs a certain amount of money each day.

Development cost, on the other hand, is harder to determine because it's more difficult to estimate the complexity of the system beforehand. The changes you'll encounter are hard to estimate in advance, and hence the cost is hard to estimate as well.

Project Goal Fulfilled

This is also a tricky criterion, because what does *goal fulfillment* really mean? Does it mean all requirements set at the beginning of a project are fulfilled? Or does it mean the system, when delivered, contains the things the end user wants (and thing they may not want)?

Most surveys seem to take the traditional approach: requirements are set early and never change. But what about the problems you saw earlier with complex projects? Can you really know all the requirements from the start? Something that we think everybody who has participated in a software project can agree on is that requirements change during the course of a project, period!

It might very well be that all the requirements you knew about from the start have been implemented, but things have changed so much during the project that the users still don't think the project has delivered any value. The project could be seen as successful because it has fulfilled its scope, but is it really successful if the users don't get a system they're satisfied with? Have you truly delivered business value to your customer? *That* is what you should have as a goal.

Throughout the development process, you need to identify the business value you deliver and make sure you do deliver it. The business value might not be obvious from the start of the project, but it should be focused on during the process. A good development process and ALM process can help you achieve this.

Let's now take a look at the factors that influence project success.

Factors Influencing Projects and Their Success

As we've said, today's enterprises face a lot of new challenges. Let's go through some of them in more detail, starting with the most important one based on our own experience.

The Gap between Business and IT

Let's start with the biggest issue. IT managers' top priority has often been better integration between the company's business processes and the supporting IT systems. There seems to be quite a collaboration gap between the IT side and the business side, making it difficult to deliver software and systems that really do support the business. IT managers may focus on security, scalability, or availability instead of on supporting business processes. These are of course important as well, but they aren't the only issues IT should focus on. Business managers, on the other hand, may have trouble explaining what they want from the systems. This collaboration gap poses a great threat not only for projects but also for the entire company.

The Development Process—Or the Lack of One

Let's continue with the development process. Can this affect success? Obviously, it can. We've seen organizations that spent lots of effort, time, and money on developing a good process, and that trained project managers and participants in RUP, XP, or any other development model they chose, and you would think all was dandy—but projects suffered. One reason might be that when a project starts, it's hard to follow the process. RUP, for instance, is often said to be too extensive, with many documents to write and milestones to meet. Let's face it—even Ivar Jacobson, creator of RUP, seems to think this, considering his latest process development like the Scaled Agile Framework (SAFe).

If the process is seen as a problem or a burden, project members will find ways around it, and the money spent on training and planning will be wasted. The process may also be hard to implement because the tools have no way of supporting it. If you can't integrate your development process into the tools you use to perform work, you most likely won't follow the process. Using the process must be easy, and the tools should make the process as transparent as it can be, so that you can focus on work but still follow the process.

When Joachim and his coworkers travel around Sweden talking to organizations about ALM, they usually ask what development process the organizations use. Often the answer is "the chaos model," or "the cowboy model," meaning they use a lot of ad hoc, often manual, efforts to keep it all going. Many say this is due to an inability to integrate their real development model into their tools, but others haven't given it a thought. Such companies have barely considered using any work structure; and if they have, the thoughts often stay in the heads of the developers (who often are the ones longing for a good process) or managers. Maybe a decision was made to consider training staff in a model, but the company never got around to it. No wonder these organizations experience lots of failed or challenged projects.

Speaking of processes, not having a flexible development process most definitely affects project success. Because your business is sure to change during a development project, you need to be flexible in your process so that you can catch these changes and deliver business value in the end. We had a discussion with a customer about this some time ago. Most customers agree that there must be a way to make it easier to catch changes to requirements and make the system better reflect reality during a project. Otherwise, the perceived value of the project suffers. But in this case, the IT manager seemed scared to even consider this. He argued that all requirements must be known at the start of the project and that they must remain static throughout the project. He thought the project would never reach an end otherwise. Not a single argument could break down his wall. He wanted to run his company's projects by using the Waterfall model (see Chapter 3), as he always had. And still he kept wondering why projects so often ended badly.

Geographic Spread

With development spread across the globe and outsourced development, running projects can be very hard indeed. When development teams involved in a project are geographically separated, means of communication between them must exist and function seamlessly. For example, how can you share project status in an effective way, so that everybody can see how the project is going? How can you achieve good, robust version control for source code and documents? How can you catch changes to requirements when users, developers, and decision makers are separated?

This complexity is something we've seen in a recent project at a global company in the dental business. The organization has development teams in Sweden, Belgium, the United States, and Canada. This causes headaches from time to time, especially when teams need to collaborate or communicate. This company lacks a clear strategy for how to improve the ALM process, but it's taking steps to get the process going. So far the improvements are pointing in the right direction, so the company has decided to continue the project.

Such complexity takes its toll on scrum masters, product owners, traditional project managers, and the projects themselves. Tools and processes must be in place to support the project teams. Obviously, both time and cost can be severely negatively affected by geographic separation. If you don't catch requirements changes, fulfillment of project scope (or the perceived added value of the project) will most likely suffer, increasing the risk that the project will fail (or at least be severely challenged).

Synchronization of Tools

Numerous times, we've seen situations where a developer (or other team member) must use several tools to get the job done. This poses a problem for developers, especially if they work in teams. (A single developer might not have these problems.)

Suppose there is one tool for writing code, one for bug reporting, one for testing, one for version control, one for reports and statistics, and so on. We're sure you recognize this situation. The coordination required to keep all information in sync between these systems is immense—not to mention the difficulties of implementing a development process using all of them, if this is even possible in all the systems.

There are good integrated toolsets on the market that enable you to minimize context switching. Such tools have the same or a similar GUI whether you're a developer or a tester or are performing another role. Other tools integrate seamlessly, also minimizing the strain of context switching.

Resource Management

What about *Project Portfolio Management (PPM*; see Figure 1-2)? Keeping track of all running projects and their resources can be a considerable problem for enterprises. The investments in applications and projects are enormous, whether from a financial perspective or from a human capital perspective. PPM helps organizations balance the costs and values of IT investments so they can achieve their business goals.[2]

---

[2]Kelly A. Shaw, "Application Lifecycle Management and PPM," June 2007, www.serena.com.

Figure 1-2. *What PPM is about*

One big independent research company, Forrester, says "PPM provides a fact-based process for evaluating, prioritizing, and monitoring projects. PPM unites the process of strategic planning, resource and budget allocation, project selection and implementation, and post-project metrics."[3]

This basically says it all about the issues covered by PPM.

You can also see that a great portion of IT investments are focused on custom application development. If you can't manage the resources you have at your disposal, the projects will most definitely suffer. You need to know, for example, that Steve will be available at the time he is needed for your project according to your project plan. If he isn't, the schedule might have to change, and the project most likely will be affected by both time and cost increases. To make matters worse, tasks depending on Steve's work may suffer as well. This issue is one of our customers' top priorities now. Many of the questions we get when speaking about TFS implementations concern resource management integration with TFS.

Project Size

Project size can also affect project outcomes. This is perhaps no surprise, because complexity usually increases when project size increases. It's hard to manage a project that has many people involved or a long timeline. If you combine a large project size with geographically spread project teams or members, keeping it all from falling apart becomes difficult, and it's harder to foresee everything that can happen. Of course, all software development is difficult and involves risks, but these factors tend to make it harder and riskier.

[3]Craig Symons with Bobby Cameron, Laurie Orlov, Lauren Sessions, Forrester Research, "How IT Must Shape and Manage Demand," June 2006, http://www.techrepublic.com/resource-library/whitepapers/forrester-best-practices-how-it-must-shape-and-manage-demand/.

Project Success: What Does the Research Say?

When we discuss this topic with coworkers, many have views and opinions, but not many can reference research directly. Rather, they argue based on a gut feeling. This section covers some of the research about project success over the years. We examine a well-known report from the Standish Group and some disagreements with this report.

The Standish Report

The Standish Group performs a survey on a regular basis on the performance of IT projects in the United States and Europe. The first report, in 1994, was quite famous: it showed that many IT projects were cancelled or severely challenged.

In 2009, the figures looked like this (see also Figure 1-3)[4]:

- 44% of projects were challenged (53% in 1994), meaning they were late, over budget, and/or had less than the required features and functions.

- 24% of projects failed (31% in 1994), meaning they were cancelled prior to completion or delivered and never used.

- 32% were successful (16% in 1994), meaning they were delivered on time, on budget, and with required features and functions.

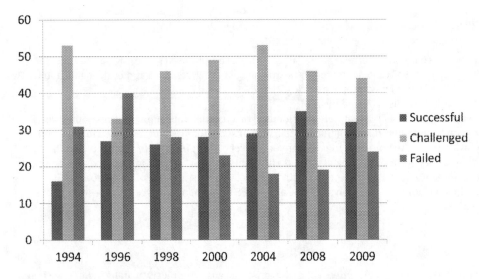

Figure 1-3. *The Standish report from 2009 shows figures from 1994 forward*

The figures have improved a little over the years, although still many projects seem to be unsuccessful in some way. The values improved in the 2011 report as well. But to us, lumping failed and challenged IT projects together isn't quite correct. Just because a project is challenged doesn't mean it hasn't added value to the company. A project might be late or overrun its budget but still deliver great value to the company, which makes it a well-received project anyway. Keep this in mind when you see figures like the preceding ones—a little perspective doesn't hurt.

---

[4]The Standish Group International, "Chaos Summary 2009," www.standishgroup.com/newsroom/chaos_2009.php.

Before we leave the Standish report, let's look at what it says about the reasons for project success. These are interesting regardless of whether you believe in the actual project-success figures. Here are the Standish Group's top ten reasons for project success:[5]

- User involvement

- Executive management support

- Clear business objectives

- Optimizing scope

- Agile process

- Project manager expertise

- Financial management

- Skilled resources

- Formal methodology

- Standard tools and infrastructure

These are interesting reasons. Most of them can be helped by implementing a good ALM process and a good integrated ALM toolset.

Challenging the Report

The figures from the Standish Group have been challenged by other researchers. Robert C. Glass wrote an interesting article that questions where the Standish report's data really comes from.[6] He also questions the methods used by the Standish Group. Glass asks you to stand back and ask yourself two things:

- Does the report represent reality?

- Is it supported by research findings?

Glass asks these questions because many other academic studies and guru reports in this area reference the Standish report from 1994. However, these other studies don't present much new material to support the old findings, according to Glass. Another problem is that the Standish Group doesn't describe its research process or indicate where its data came from so that others can discuss its validity. This is of course a huge problem.

Conclusions

So what do surveys and statistics tell us? Well, the limited data suggests that projects aren't carried out in the most optimal way. There are still too many challenged and abandoned projects in this day and age. These figures are worrying and, in our opinion, something that a serious development organization should consider and discuss internally.

We can also say from experience that too many IT projects tend to be less than perfect. Over the years, we've seen the issues discussed in this chapter in many organizations. This is one of the top reasons we wanted to work with ALM: we wanted to help organizations change and work in a better way.

---

[5]Deborah Hartmann, "Interview: Jim Johnson of the Standish Group," 2006, www.infoq.com/articles/Interview-Johnson-Standish-CHAOS.

[6]Robert C. Glass, "The Standish Report: Does It Really Describe a Software Crisis?" August 2006, *Communications of the ACM.* www.uio.no/studier/emner/matnat/ifi/INF5180/v10/undervisningsmateriale/reading-materials/p01/glass.pdf

If your ALM process is flawed, most of your projects will suffer. You should take control of the ALM process so you can deliver better projects: having an overall process helps you. And with this process comes a mindset focused on the application, all the way from its birth as a business need to the delivered business value. The importance of an overall ALM process is that it can help you better control the project outcome, enabling you to deliver true business value.

Measuring project success or failure is complicated. You need to take this into consideration when you read surveys stating that this or that many projects succeed. You need to reflect on the results of surveys before you take them as the truth. This doesn't mean the survey discussed in this section is without value. It definitely indicates that something is wrong with the way IT projects are performed today. Why do so many IT projects fail? The IT industry has been around for quite some time, and we should have learned something along the way, shouldn't we?

Could it be because the problems we need to solve keep getting harder? Or is it so difficult to estimate and plan for projects that we can only make an educated guess at the beginning of a project? If the latter is true, why do we still measure a project's success based on time, money, and requirements fulfillment? Maybe we should shift our focus to business value, instead. If the business value is greater than the cost of implementing the solution, the time and money (cost) required for the project are usually of less importance.

Summary

An alarmingly large portion of IT projects delivered today are challenged or, in the worst case, abandoned. Many projects have overruns in terms of cost and time. Projects are also criticized for not delivering business value, and hence they aren't what the customer expects them to be in the end. One issue is the lack of integration between the business side and the IT side; this gap makes it harder to deliver what you should deliver in a project, which is business value. Having a development process that is ill-defined or not used is another problem. Furthermore, the lack of mature ALM tools makes it difficult to deliver, especially because there are more geographically dispersed development and project teams these days. Much of the money spent on these projects is thrown away because of these challenges.

The problems addressed in this chapter can be dealt with if you have control of your entire ALM process. This process, as you see in the next chapter, focuses on taking business needs and requirements and turning them into business value for the organization. ALM does so by enforcing a process for how you work when developing software.

This book shows you how to take control of the ALM process. The result is that you can reduce the impact of the problems presented in this chapter.

Now it's time to look more closely at the concept of ALM. Chapter 2 covers many aspects of ALM and why it's more than just the software-development lifecycle.

CHAPTER 2

■ ■ ■

Introduction to Application Lifecycle Management

What do you think about when you hear the term *Application Lifecycle Management (ALM)*? During a seminar tour in 2005 in Sweden, presenting on Microsoft Visual Studio Team System, we asked people what ALM was and whether they cared about it. To our surprise, many people equated ALM with operations and maintenance. This is still often the case when we visit companies, although more today are aware of the term.

Was that your answer as well? Does ALM include more than just operations? Yes, it does. ALM is the thread that ties together the development lifecycle. It involves all the steps necessary to coordinate development lifecycle activities. Operations are just one part of the ALM process. Other elements range from requirements gathering to more technical things like the build and deploy process.

Aspects of the ALM Process

All software development includes various steps performed by people playing specific roles. There are many different roles, or disciplines, in the ALM process, and we define some of them in this section. (The process could include more roles, but we focus on the primary ones.)

Look at Figure 2-1, which illustrates ALM and some of its aspects. You can see the flow from the birth of an application, when the business need first arises, to when the business need no longer exists and the application dies. Once the thought of a new application (or system) is born, many organizations do some portfolio rationalization. This means you discuss whether an existing system can handle the need or if a new system has to be developed. If a new system must be built, you enter the *software development lifecycle (SDLC)* and develop the system, test it, and deploy it into operation. This is the point at which you do a handover so that Operations can maintain and refine the system. Once in production, the system (hopefully) delivers the intended business value until retirement. While in operation, the system usually is updated or undergoes bug fixes; at such times, *change requests (CRs)* are written. For each CR, you go through the same process again.

ALM Process & Roles

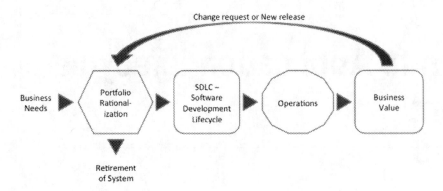

Figure 2-1. *The Application Lifecycle Management process*

It's essential to understand that all business software development is a team effort. The roles collaborate on projects in order to deliver business value to the organization. If you don't have this collaboration, the value of the system most likely will be considerably lower than it could be. One step up from the project level, it's also important to have collaboration between all roles involved in the ALM process, so that you perform this process in the most optimal way.

The roles in the ALM process include, but aren't limited to, the following:

- *Stakeholders*: Stakeholders are usually the people who either pay for the project or have decision-making rights about what to build. We like to also include end users in this group so not only management has a stake in a project.

- *Business manager*: Somebody has to decide that a development activity is going to start. After initial analysis of the business needs, a business manager decides to initiate a project to develop an application or system that will deliver the expected business value. A business manager, for instance, must be involved in the approval process for a new suggested project, including portfolio rationalization, before a decision to go ahead is made. IT managers are also part of this process, of course, because IT staff will probably be involved in the project's development and deployment into the infrastructure.

- *Project manager, product owner, or scrum master*: Suitable individuals are selected to fill these roles, and they set to work on the project after the decision to go ahead is made. Ideally, these people continue leading the project all the way through, so that you have continuity in project management.

- *Project Management Office (PMO) decision makers*: These individuals are also involved in planning, because a new project may change or expand the company's portfolio.

- *Business analyst*: After requirements collection starts, the business analyst has much to do. Usually, initial requirements are gathered when the business need arises, but the real work often begins after portfolio rationalization. A business analyst is responsible for analyzing the business needs and requirements of the stakeholders, to help identify business problems and propose solutions. Within the system's development lifecycle, the business analyst typically performs a collaborative function between the business side of an enterprise and the providers of services to the enterprise.

CHAPTER 2 ▦ INTRODUCTION TO APPLICATION LIFECYCLE MANAGEMENT

- *Architect*: The architect draws an initial picture of the solution. We don't go into detail here, because Chapter 4 does that. But briefly, the architect draws the blueprint of the system, and the system designers or engineers use this blueprint. The blueprint includes the level of freedom necessary in the system: scalability, hardware replacement, new user interfaces, and so on. The architect must consider all these issues.

- *User experience (UX) design team*: UX design should be a core deliverable and not something you leave to the developers to handle. Unfortunately, it's often overlooked; it should be given more consideration. It's important to have close collaboration between the UX team (which could be just one person) and the development team. The best solution is obviously to have a UX expert on the development team throughout the project, but sometimes that isn't possible. The UX design is important in making sure users can perceive the value of the system. You can write the best business logic in the world, but if the UX is badly designed, users probably won't think the system is any good.

- *Database administrators (DBAs)*: Almost every business system or application uses a database in some way. DBAs can make your databases run like lightning with good up-time, so it's essential to use their expertise in any project involving a database. Be nice to them; they can give you lots of tips about how to make a smarter system. Alas for DBAs, developers handle this work more and more frequently. This means developers are expected to have vertical knowledge and not just focus on coding.

- *Developers*: "Developers, developers, developers!" as Microsoft CEO Steve Ballmer shouted in a famous video. And who can blame him? These are the people working their magic to realize the system by using the architecture blueprint drawn from the requirements. Moreover, developers modify or extend the code when change requests come in.

- *Testers*: We'd rather not see testing as a separate activity. Don't get us wrong: it's a role, but testing is something you should consider from the first time you write down a requirement and continue doing during the whole process. Testers and test managers help you secure quality, but modern development practices include testing by developers as well. For instance, in Test Driven Development (TDD), developers write tests that can be automated and run at build time or as part of checking in to version control.

- *Operations and maintenance staff*: When an application or system is finished, it's handed over to operations. The operations staff takes care of it until it retires, often with the help of the original developers, who come in to do bug fixes and new upgrades. Don't forget to involve these people early in the process, at the point when the initial architecture is considered, and keep them involved with the project until everything is done. They can provide great input about what can and can't be done within the company infrastructure. So, operations is just one part—although an important one—of ALM. In Chapter 9 this book talks about DevOps, which is a practice that ties developers and operations more closely.

All project efforts are done collaboratively. No role can act separately from the others if you're to succeed with any project. It's essential for everybody involved to have a collaborative mindset and to have the business value as their primary focus at every phase of the project.

If you're part of an agile development process, such as a Scrum project, you might have only three roles: product owner, scrum master, and team members. This doesn't mean the roles just described don't apply, though! They're all essential in most projects; it's just that in an agile project, you may not be labeled a developer or an architect. Rather, you're a team member, and you and your co-members share responsibility for the work you're doing. We go deeper into the agile world later in the book (see Chapter 4).

15

Four Ways of Looking at ALM

ALM is the glue that ties together the roles we just discussed and the activities they perform. Let's consider four ways of looking at ALM (see Figure 2-2). We've chosen these four because we've seen this separation in many of the organizations we've worked with or spoken to:

- *Software development lifecycle (SDLC) view*: This is perhaps the most common way of looking at ALM, because development has "owned" management of the application lifecycle for a long time. This could be an effect of the gap between the business side and the IT side in most organizations, and IT has taken the lead.

- *Service management or operations view*: Operations have also been (in our experience) unfortunately separated from IT development. This has resulted in Operations having its own view of ALM and the problems in this area.

- *Application Portfolio Management (APM) view*: Again, perhaps because of the gap between business and IT, we've seen many organizations with a portfolio ALM strategy in which IT development is only one small part. From a business view, the focus has been on how to handle the portfolio and not on the entire ALM process.

- *Unified view*: Fortunately, some organizations focus on the entire ALM process by including all three of the preceding views. This is the only way to take control over, and optimize, ALM. For a CIO, it's essential to have this view all the time; otherwise, things can easily get out of hand.

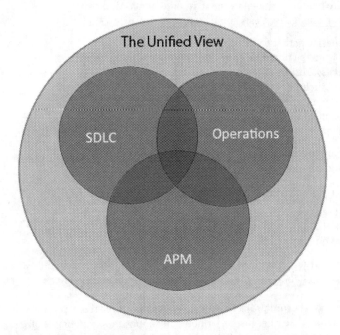

Figure 2-2. *The four ways of looking at ALM*

Let's look at these four views in more detail, starting with the SDLC view.

The SDLC View

Let's consider ALM from an SDLC perspective first. In Figure 2-3, you can see the different phases of a typical development project and the roles most frequently involved. Keep in mind that this is a simplified view for the sake of this discussion. We've also tried to fit in the different roles from the ALM process, presented earlier.

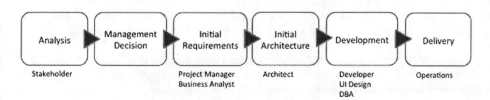

Figure 2-3. *A simplified view of a typical development project*

First, somebody comes up with an idea based on an analysis of business needs: "Hey, wouldn't it be great if we had a system that could help us do this (whatever the idea is)?" It can also be the other way around: the idea comes first, and the business value is evaluated based on the idea.

An analysis or feasibility study is performed, costs are estimated, and (hopefully) a decision is made by IT and business management to start an IT project. A project manager (PM) is selected to be responsible for the project; the PM begins gathering requirements with the help of business analysts, PMO decision makers, and users or others affected. The PM also starts planning the project in as much detail as possible at this moment.

When that is done, the architect begins looking at how to realize the new system, and the initial design is chosen. The initial design is evaluated and updated based on what happens during the project and how requirements change throughout the project. Development beings, including work performed by developers, user interface (UI) designers, and DBAs (and anyone else not mentioned here but important for the project).

Testing is, at least for us, something done all along the way—from requirements specification to delivered code—so it doesn't get a separate box in Figure 2-3; we include acceptance testing by end users or stakeholders in the Development box. After the system has gone through acceptance testing, it's delivered to Operations for use in the organization. Of course, the process doesn't end here. This cycle is generally repeated over and over as new versions are rolled out and bug fixes are implemented.

What ALM does in this development process is support the coordination of all development lifecycle activities by doing the following:

- Making sure you have processes that span these activities.

- Managing the relationships between development project artifacts used or produced by these activities (in other words, providing traceability). These artifacts include UI mockups done at requirements gathering, source code, executable code, build scripts, test plans, and so on.

- Reporting on progress of the development effort as a whole so you have transparency for everyone regarding project advancement.

As you can see, ALM doesn't support a specific activity: its purpose is to keep all activities in sync. It does this so you can focus on delivering systems that meet the needs and requirements of the business. By having an ALM process that helps you synchronize your development activities, you can more easily determine if any activity is underperforming and thus take corrective actions.

The Service Management or Operations View

From a service management or operations view, you can look at ALM as in this quote from *ITIL Application Management* by the Office of Government Commerce in United Kingdom (TSO, 2002): ALM "focuses on the activities that are involved with the deployment, operation, support, and optimization of the application. The main objective is to ensure that the application, once built and deployed, can meet the service level that has been defined for it."

When you see ALM from this perspective, it focuses on the life of an application or system in a production environment. If, in the SDLC view, the development lifecycle starts with the decision to go ahead with a project, here it starts with deployment into the production environment. Once deployed, the application is operated by the Operations crew. Bug fixes and change requests are handled by them, and they also pat it on its back to make it feel good and run smoothly.

This is a healthy way of looking at ALM in our opinion: Development and Operations are two pieces of ALM, cooperating to manage the entire ALM process. You should consider both pieces from the beginning when planning a development project; you can't have one without the other.

The Application Portfolio Management View

In the APM view of ALM, you see the application as a product managed as part of a portfolio of products. APM is a subset of Project Portfolio Management (PPM),[1] discussed in Chapter 1. Figure 2-4 illustrates this process.

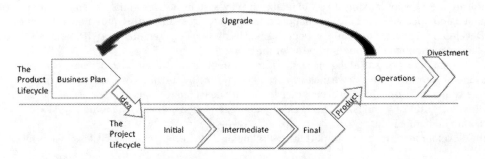

Figure 2-4. *The APM view of ALM*

This view comes from the Project Management Institute (PMI). Managing resources and the projects they work on is very important for any organization. In Figure 2-4, you can see that the product lifecycle starts with a business plan—the product is an application or system that is one part of the business plan. An idea for an application is turned into a project and carried out through the project phases until it's turned over to Operations as a finished product.

---

[1]The PMI is the world's leading not-for-profit professional membership association for the project, program, and portfolio management profession. Read more at www.pmi.org.

When business requirements change or a new release (an upgrade, in Figure 2-4) is required for some other reason, the project lifecycle starts again, and a new release is handed over to Operations. After a while (maybe years), the system or application is discarded (this is called *divestment*, the opposite of investment). This view doesn't specifically speak about the operations part or the development part of the process but should instead be seen in the light of APM.

The Unified View

Finally, there is a unified view of ALM. In this case, an effort is made to align the previous views with the business. Here you do as the CIO would do: you focus on the business needs, not on separate views. You do this to improve the capacity and agility of a project from beginning to end. Figure 2-5 shows an overview of the unified ALM view of a business.

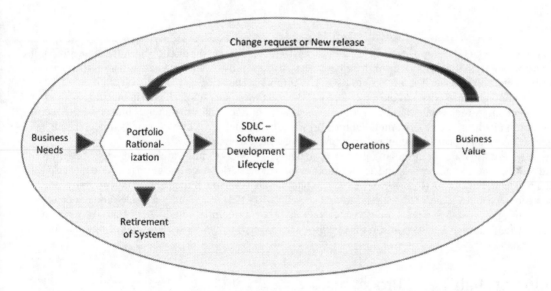

Figure 2-5. *The CIO's view takes into consideration all three views previously mentioned*

You probably recognize this figure from Figure 2-1. We want to stress that with the unified view, you need to consider all aspects from the birth to the death of an application or a system; hence the circle around the figure.

Three Pillars of Traditional Application Lifecycle Management

Let's now look at some important pillars of ALM that are independent of the view you take; see Figure 2-6. These pillars were first introduced by Forrester Research.[2]

---

[2]Dave West, "The Time Is Right For ALM 2.0+," October 19, 2010, Forrester Research, www.forrester.com/The+Time+Is+Right+For+ALM+20/fulltext/-/E-RES56832?objectid=RES56832.

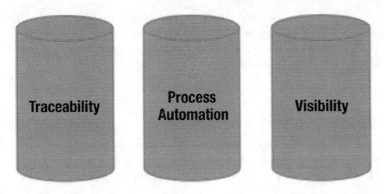

Figure 2-6. *The three pillars of ALM*

The following sections go over these pillars in greater detail, starting with traceability.

Traceability

Some customers we've seen have stopped doing upgrades on systems running in production because their companies had poor or no traceability in their systems. For these customers, it was far too expensive to do upgrades because of the unexpected effects even a small change could have. The companies had no way of knowing which original requirements were implemented where in the applications. The effect was that a small change in one part of the code might affect another part, which would come as a surprise because poor traceability meant they had no way of seeing the code connection in advance. One customers claimed (as we've heard in discussions with many other customers) that traceability can be a major cost driver in any enterprise if not done correctly.

There must be a way to trace requirements all the way to delivered code—through architect models, design models, build scripts, unit tests, test cases, and so on—not only to make it easier to go back into the system when implementing bug fixes, but also to demonstrate that the system has delivered the things the business wanted.

You also need traceability in order to achieve internal as well as external compliance with rules and regulations. If you develop applications for the medical industry, for example, you must comply with FDA regulations. You also need traceability when change requests come in so you know where you updated the system and in which version you performed the update.

Automation of High-Level Processes

The next pillar of ALM is automation of high-level processes. All organizations have processes, as you saw in Chapter 1. For example, approval processes control hand-offs between the analysis and design or build steps, or between deployment and testing. Much of this is done manually in many projects, and ALM stresses the importance of automating these tasks for a more effective and less time-consuming process. Having an automated process also decreases the error rate compared to handling the process manually.

Visibility into the Progress of Development Efforts

The third and last pillar of ALM is providing visibility into the progress of development efforts. Many managers and stakeholders have limited visibility into the progress of development projects. The visibility they have often comes from steering-group meetings, during which the project manager reviews the current situation. Some would argue that this limitation is good; but if you want an effective process, you must ensure visibility.

Other interest groups, such as project members, also have limited visibility of the entire project despite being part of the project. This is often due to the fact that reporting is difficult and can involve a lot of manual work. Daily status reports take too much time and effort to produce, especially when you have information in many repositories.

A Brief History of ALM Tools and Concepts

You can resolve the three pillars of ALM manually if you want to, without using tools or automation. (ALM isn't a new process description, even though Microsoft, IBM, HP, Atlassian, and the other big software houses are pushing ALM to drive sales of their respective ALM solutions.) You can, for instance, continue to use Excel spreadsheets or, like one of our most dedicated agile colleagues, use sticky notes and a pad of paper to track requirements through use cases/scenarios, test cases, code, build, and so on to delivered code. It works, but this process takes a lot of time and requires much manual effort. With constant pressure to keep costs down, you need to make tracking requirements more effective.

Of course, project members can simplify the process by keeping reporting to the bare minimum. With a good tool or set of tools, you can cut time (and thus costs) and effort, and still get the required traceability you want in your projects. The same goes for reporting and other activities. Tools can, in our opinion, help you be more effective and also help you automate much of the ALM process into the tool(s).

Having the process built directly into your tools helps prevent the people involved from missing important steps by simplifying things. For instance, the agile friend we mentioned could definitely gain much from this, and he is looking into Microsoft Team Foundation Server (TFS) to see how that set of tools can help him and his teams be more productive. Process automation and the use of tools to support and simplify daily jobs are great because they can keep you from making unnecessary mistakes.

Serena Software Inc. is one supplier of ALM tools, and the company has interesting insight into ALM and related concepts. According to Serena Software, there are eight ALM concepts:[3]

- *Modeling*: Software modeling

- *Issue management*: Keeping track of incoming issues during both development and operations

- *Design*: Designing the system or application

- *Construction*: Developing the system or application

- *Production monitoring*: The work of the Operations staff

- *Build*: Building the executable code

- *Test*: Testing the software

- *Release management*: Planning application releases

In order to synchronize these, according to Serena Software, you need tools that span them and that help you automate and simplify the following activities. If you look closely, you can see that these activities compare to ALM 2.0+, which we discuss shortly:

- Reporting

- Traceability

- Policies

- Procedures

- Processes

- Collaboration

Imagine the Herculean task of keeping all those things in order manually. It's impossible, if you want to get things right and keep an eye on the project's status. As you saw when we discussed the Standish Group's report in Chapter 1, projects today seem to be going better because the number of failed projects is decreasing. Much of this

---

[3]Kelly A. Shaw, Ph.D, "Application Lifecycle Management for the Enterprise," Serena Software Inc, April 2007, www.serena.com/docs/repository/company/serena_alm_2.0_for_t.pdf.

progress is, according to Michael Azoff at the Butler Group,[4] the result of "major changes in software development: open source software projects; the Agile development movement; and advances in tooling, notably Application Lifecycle Management (ALM) tools." Some of these results have also been confirmed by later research, such as that by Scott W. Ambler at Ambysoft.[5] Now you understand why finding tools and development processes to help you with ALM is important.

There is increasing awareness of the ALM process among enterprises. We see this among our customers. ALM is much more important now than it was only five years ago.

Application Lifecycle Management 1.0

Forrester Research has introduced some very useful concepts for ALM,[6] including different versions of ALM and ALM tools. This section looks at how Forrester defined ALM 1.0 and then continues to the latest version, ALM 2.0+.

As software has become more and more complex, role specialization has increased in IT organizations. This has led to functional silos in different areas (roles), such as project management, business analysis, architecture, development, database administration, testing, and so on. As you may recall from the beginning of this chapter, you can see this in the ALM circle. Having these silos in a company isn't a problem, but having them without any positive interaction between them is an issue.

There is always a problem when you build impenetrable walls around you. ALM vendors have driven this wall construction, because most of their tools historically have been developed for particular silos. For example, if you look at build-management tools, they have supported the build silo (naturally) but have little or no interaction with test and validation tools (which is strange because the first thing that usually happens in a test cycle is the build). This occurs despite the fact that interaction between roles can generate obvious synergies with great potential. You need to synchronize the ALM process to make the role-centric processes part of the overall process. This might sound obvious, but it hasn't happened until recently.

Instead of having complete integration between the roles or disciplines mentioned at the start of the chapter, and the tools they use, there has been point-to-point integration—for example, a development tool is slightly integrated with a testing tool (or, probably, the other way around). Each tool uses its own data repository, so traceability and reporting are hard to handle in such an environment as well (see Figure 2-7).

---

[4]Michael Azoff, "Application Lifecycle Management Making a Difference," February 2007, Enterprise Networks and Services, OpinionWire.
[5]"2011 IT Project Success Rates Survey Results," www.ambysoft.com/surveys/success2011.html.
[6]West, "The Time Is Right For ALM 2.0+."

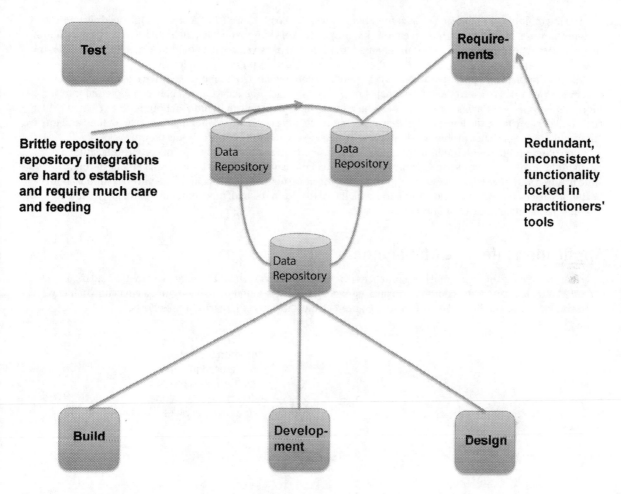

Figure 2-7. *ALM 1.0*

This point-to-point integration makes the ALM process fragile and expensive. However, this isn't just a characteristic of ALM 1.0—it's true for all integrations. Imagine that one tool is updated or replaced: the integration may break, and new solutions have to be found to get it working again. This scenario can be a reality if, for example, old functions in the updated or replaced tool are obsolete and the new tool doesn't support backward compatibility. What would happen if Microsoft Word (to take an easy example) suddenly stopped supporting older Word files? There would be more or less a riot among users until the situation was fixed. This can be hard to solve even with integration between two tools. What if you have a more complex situation, including several tools? We've seen projects using six or seven tools during development, creating a fragile solution when new versions are released.

Tools have also been centered on one discipline. In real life, a project member working as a developer, for instance, often also acts as an architect or a tester. Because the people in each of these disciplines have their own tool (or set of tools), the project member must use several tools and switch between them. It could also be that the task system is separated from the rest of the tools, so to start working on a task, a developer must first retrieve the task from the task system—perhaps they must print it out, or copy and paste it, then open the requirements system to check the requirement, then look at the architecture in that system, and finally open the development tool to begin working. Hopefully the testing tools are integrated into the development tool; otherwise, yet another tool must be used. All this switching costs valuable time that could be better put into solving the task.

Having multiple tools for each project member is obviously costly as well, because everyone needs licenses for the tools they use. Even with open source tools that may be free of charge, you have maintenance costs, adaptions of the tools, developer costs, and so on. Maintenance can be very expensive, so you shouldn't forget this even when the tools are free. Such a scenario can be very costly and very complex. It's probably also fragile.

As an example, take two co-workers at a large medical company in Gothenburg. They have a mix of tools in their everyday work. We asked them to estimate how much time they needed to switch between tools and transfer information from one tool to another. They estimated that they spend half an hour to an hour each day syncing their work. Usually they're on the lower end of that scale, but in the long run all the switching takes a lot of time and money. Our friends also experience problems whenever they need to upgrade any of the systems they use.

One other problem with traditional ALM tools that's worth mentioning is that vendors often add features: for example, adapting a test tool to support issue and defect management. In the issue-management system, some features may have been added to support testing. Because neither tool has enough features to support both disciplines, users are confused and don't know which tool to use. In the end, most purchase both, just to be safe, and end up with the integration issues described earlier.

Application Lifecycle Management 2.0

Let's look at what the emerging tools and practices (including processes and methodologies) in ALM 2.0 try to do for you. ALM is a platform for the coordination and management of development activities, not a collection of lifecycle tools with locked-in and limited ALM features. Figure 2-8 and Table 2-1 summarize these efforts.

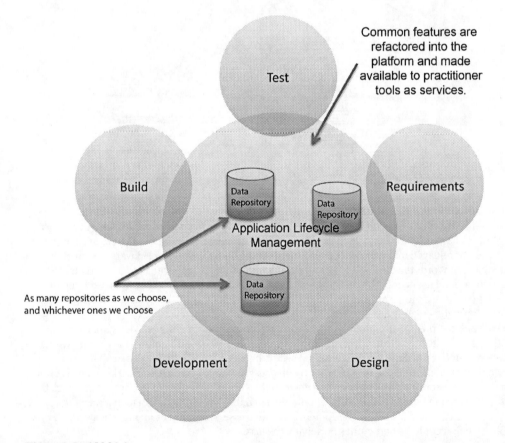

Figure 2-8. ALM 2.0

Table 2-1. *Characteristics of ALM 2.0*

Characteristic	Benefit
Practitioner tools assembled from plug-ins	Customers pay only for the features they need. Practitioners find the features they need more quickly.
Common services available across practitioner tools	Easier for vendors to deploy enhancements to shared features. Ensures correspondence of activities across practitioner tools.
Repository neutral	No need to migrate old assets. Better support for cross-platform development.
Use of open integration standards	Easier for customers and partners to build deeper integrations with third-party tools.
Microprocesses and macroprocesses governed by an externalized workflow	Processes are versionable assets. Processes can share common components.

One of the first things you can see is a focus on plug-ins. This means from one tool, you can add the features you need to perform the tasks you want, without using several tools! If you've used Visual Studio, you've seen that it's straightforward to add new plug-ins to the development environment. Support for Windows Communication Foundation (WCF) and Windows Presentation Services, for example, was available as plug-ins long before support for them was added as part of Visual Studio 2008.

Having the plug-in option and making it easy for third-party vendors to write plug-ins for the tool greatly eases the integration problems discussed earlier. You can almost compare this to a smorgasbord, where you choose the things you want. So far this has mostly been adopted by development tool vendors such as IBM and Microsoft, but more plug-ins are coming. IBM has its Rational suite of products, and Microsoft has TFS. Chapter 11 looks at them more closely.

Teamprise, a third-party vendor, developed a solution that gives access to TFS from a wide array of platforms, including Mac OS X (see Figure 2-9). In November 2009, Teamprise was acquired by Microsoft. After the acquisition, TFS 2010 changed its name to Team Explorer Everywhere. In writing this book, we used Team Explorer Everywhere on our Mac OS X laptops and used the Eclipse development platform for many examples.

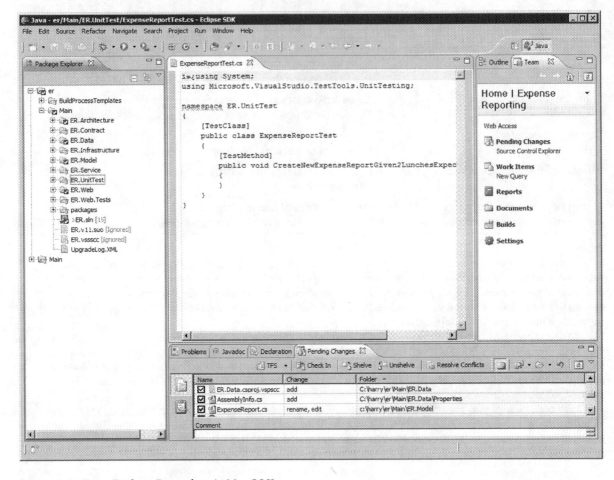

Figure 2-9. *Team Explorer Everywhere in Mac OS X*

Another thing that eases development efforts is that vendors in ALM 2.0 focus more on identifying features common to multiple tools and integrating them into the ALM platform, including the following:

- Collaboration

- Workflow

- Security

- Reporting and analysis

Another goal of ALM 2.0 is that the tools should be repository neutral. There should be not a single repository but many, so you aren't required to use the storage solution that the vendor proposes. IBM, for example, has declared that its forthcoming ALM solution will integrate with a wide variety of repositories, such as Concurrent Versions System (CVS) and Subversion, just to mention two. This approach removes the obstacle of gathering and synchronizing data, giving you easier access to progress reports, and so on. Microsoft uses an extensive set of web services and plug-ins to solve the same issue. It has one storage center (SQL Server); but by exposing functionality through the use of web services, Microsoft has made it fairly easy to connect to other tools as well.

An open and extensible ALM solution lets companies integrate their own choice of repository into the ALM tool. Both Microsoft and IBM have solutions—data warehouse adapters—that enable existing repositories to be tied into the ALM system. A large organization that has invested in tools and repositories probably doesn't want to change everything for a new ALM system; hence it's essential to have this option. Any way you choose to solve the problem will work, giving you the possibility of having a well-connected and synchronized ALM platform.

Furthermore, ALM 2.0 focuses on being built on an open integration standard. As you know, Microsoft exposes TFS functionality through web services. This isn't publicly documented and isn't supported by Microsoft, however, so you need to do some research and go through some trial and error in order to get it working. This way, you can support new tools as long as they also use an open standard; and third-party vendors have the option of writing cool and productive tools.

Process support built in to the ALM platform is another important feature. By this we mean having automated support for the ALM process built right into the tool(s). You can, for instance, have the development process (RUP, scrum, XP, and so on) automated in the tool, reminding you of each step in the process so you don't miss creating and maintaining any deliverables or checkpoints.

In the case of TFS, this support includes having the document structure, including templates for all documents, available on the project web site as soon as a new TFS project is created. You can also imagine a tool with built-in capabilities that help you with requirements gathering and specification, for instance—letting you add requirements and specs to the tool and have them transformed into tasks that are assigned to the correct role without your having to do this manually.

An organization isn't likely to scrap a way of working just because the new ALM tool says it can't import that specific process. A lot of money has often been invested in developing a process, and an organization won't want to spend the same amount again learning a new one. With ALM 2.0, it's possible to store the ALM process in a readable format such as XML.

The benefits include the fact that the process can be easily modified, version controlled, and reported on. The ALM platform can then import the process and execute the application development process descriptions in it. Microsoft, for example, uses XML to store the development process in TFS. The process XML file describes the entire ALM process, and many different process files can coexist. This means you can choose which process template you want to base your project on when creating a new project.

As you saw earlier, it's important for an enterprise to have control over its project portfolio, to better allocate and control resources. So far, none of the ALM vendors have integrated this support into the ALM platform. There may be good reasons, though. For instance, although portfolio management may require data from ALM, the reverse probably isn't the case. The good thing is that having a standards-based platform makes integration with PPM tools much easier.

Application Lifecycle Management 2.0+

So far, not all ALM 2.0 features have been implemented by most of the major ALM tool vendors. There are various reasons. One is that it isn't easy for any company to move to a single integrated suite, no matter how promising the benefits may appear. Making such a switch means changing the way you work in your development processes and maybe even throughout your company. Companies have invested in tools and practices, and spending time and money on a new platform can require considerably more investment.

For Microsoft-focused development organizations, the switch might not be as difficult, however—at least, not for the developers. They already use Visual Studio, SharePoint, and many other applications in their daily life, and the switch isn't that great. But Microsoft isn't the only platform out there, and competitors like IBM, Serena, and HP still have some work to do to convince the market.

In addition, repository-neutral standards and services haven't evolved over time. Microsoft, for instance, still relies on SQL Server as a repository and hasn't built in much support for other databases or services. The same goes for most competition to TFS.

■ **Note** Virtually all vendors use ALM tools to lock in customers to as many of their products as possible—especially *expensive* major strategic products like RDBMS. After all, these companies live mostly on license sales.

The growth of agile development and project management in recent years has also changed the way ALM must support development teams and organizations. There has been a clear change from requirements specs to backlog-driven work, and the tooling you use needs to support this.

It becomes critical for ALM tools to support agile practices such as build-and-test automation. TDD is being used with increasing frequency, and more and more developers require their tools to support this way of working. If the tools don't do that, they're of little use to an agile organization. Microsoft has taken the agile way of working to heart in the development of TFS; this book shows you all you need to know about TFS's support for agile practices.

There has also been a move from traditional project management toward an agile view where the product owner and scrum master require support from the tools. Backlog grooming (the art of grooming requirements in the agile world), agile estimation and planning, and reporting—important to these roles—need to be integrated to the overall ALM solution.

The connection between operations and maintenance also becomes more and more important. ALM tools should integrate with the tools used by these parts of the organization.

In the report "The Time Is Right for ALM 2.0+," Forrester research presented the ALM 2.0+ concept, illustrated in Figure 2-10.[7] This report extended traditional ALM with what Forrester called ALM 2.0+. Traditional ALM covers traceability, reporting, and process automation, as you've seen. Forrester envisions the future of ALM also including collaboration and work planning.

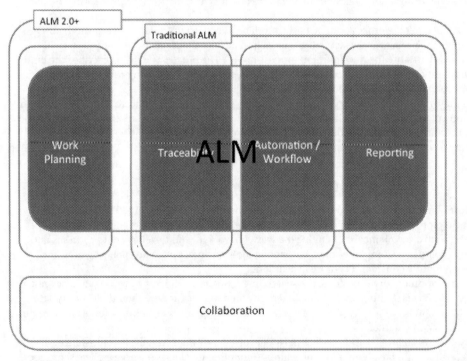

Figure 2-10. *Future ALM, according to Forrester Research*

---

[7]West, "The Time Is Right For ALM 2.0+."

These concepts are essential throughout the rest of this book: a chapter is dedicated to each one except for traceability and visibility that are combined into one chapter since they are closely related. The book's focus is on ALM 2.0+, but it includes some other older concepts as well. We've already looked at the first three cornerstones, but let's briefly examine the two new ones introduced in ALM 2.0+:

- *Work planning*: In this concept Forrester includes planning functions, such as defining tasks and allocating them to resources. These planning functions shouldn't replace the strategic planning functions that enterprise architecture and portfolio-management tools provide. Instead, they help you execute and provide feedback on those strategic plans. Integration of planning into ALM 2.0+ helps you follow up on projects so you can obtain estimates and effort statistics, which are essential to all projects.

- *Collaboration*: This is essential, as mentioned in Chapter 1. ALM 2.0+ tools must support the distributed development environment that exists in many organizations. The tools must help team members work effectively—sharing, collaborating, and interacting as if they were collocated. The tools should also do this without adding complexity to the work environment.

We take a closer look at these topics further down the road. But before that, we examine a new topic on the horizon: DevOps, which is important because it has the potential to solve many ALM problems.

DevOps

The last couple of years have seen the concept of DevOps emerge. In our view, DevOps is close to, or even the same as, the unified view of ALM presented earlier in the chapter. One big difference compared to a more traditional approach is that DevOps brings development and operations staff closer not just in thought but also physically. Because they're all part of the DevOps team, there is no handover from one part to the other—team members work together to deliver business value through continuous development and operations. Figure 2-11 shows how Microsoft looks at DevOps.

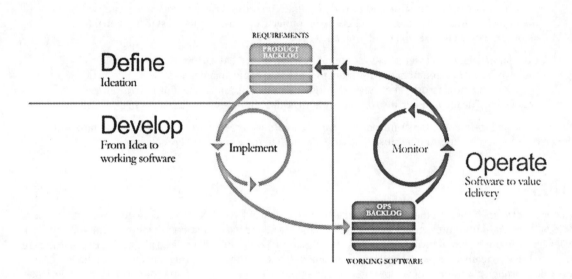

Figure 2-11. *DevOps according to Microsoft*

DevOps isn't a method on its own; instead, it uses known agile methods and processes like Kanban and Scrum, which are popular in many IT organizations. Basically, these are project-management methods based on agile concepts and are used for development (mostly Scrum) and operations (mostly Kanban). The key concepts are continuous development, continuous integration, and continuous operations. What is important is working with small changes instead of large releases (which minimizes risk), getting rid of manual steps by automating processes, and having development and test environments that are as close as possible to the production environment.

The purpose of DevOps is to optimize the time from the development of an application until it's running stably in the production environment. The quicker you can get from idea to production, the quicker you can respond to changes in, and influences from, the market—which is crucial in order to have a successful business.

Before moving to the next chapter, we present a short introduction to ALM and PPM.

ALM and PPM

ALM and PPM can support each other well. Data from the ALM repository can be an excellent source of data for the PPM tool, and hence decisions can be based on the results of the PPM tool. This requires a (one-way) working connection between the two, of course. Manual efforts involving cutting and pasting information aren't good enough because they're slow and error prone. A good integration between the two repositories gives project portfolio decision-makers access to accurate and timely data. This eases their decision-making process.

Gartner identifies five key activities in the PPM decision process that benefit from working integration:[8]

- Review current projects and their status.

- Review the application portfolio's impact on resources (which resources are available and when they're available, for instance).

- Present new capital requests. (Do we need to add more resources to a project?)

- Reprioritize the portfolio.

- Examine investments for effectiveness (basically, reviewing the outcome of projects within six months of delivery).

A lot of data important for these activities can be found in the ALM repository.

Microsoft's solution to ALM/PPM integration has room for improvement but works well. Microsoft Enterprise Project Management (EPM; `http://www.microsoft.com/project/en/gb/solutions.aspx`) is Microsoft's end-to-end collaborative project and portfolio environment. This solution aims to help organizations gain visibility, insight, and control across all work, enhancing decision making, improving alignment with business strategy, maximizing resource utilization, and measuring and helping to increase operations efficiency. We don't delve into the specifics of this solution here but will tell you a little about its three parts.

First is Microsoft Office Project Professional. If you're a project manager, chances are you know this product already. If not, you have probably seen the Gantt schema a project manager has produced. You can use Project Professional as a stand-alone product for single projects. But the real value comes when you connect it to the second part of the Microsoft EPM solution: Microsoft Office Project Server. This offers resource management, scheduling, reporting, and collaboration capabilities. You can use Project Server to store project and resource information in a central repository.

The third part of Microsoft's EPM suite used to be Microsoft Office Project Portfolio Server. Since version 2010, this is built in to Microsoft Project Server. This gives you a management solution, enabling organizations to get control of their product portfolios so that they best align with business strategies.

All in all, Microsoft Office Project Professional can help you handle your portfolios, projects, and resources so you can plan your needs.

Summary

This chapter has presented an overview of what ALM aims for and what it takes for the ALM platform to support a healthy ALM process. You've seen that ALM is the coordination and synchronization of all development lifecycle activities. There are four ways of looking at it:

- Software Development Lifecycle (SDLC) view

- Service management or operations view

- Application Portfolio Management (APM) view

- Unified view

---

[8]"Application Lifecycle Management and PPM," Serena, 2006,
`http://www.serena.com/docs/repository/alm/alm-ppm-white-paper.pdf`.

Traceability, automation of high-level processes, and visibility into development processes are three pillars of ALM. Other key components are collaboration, work planning, workflow, security, reporting, analytics, being open-standards based, being plug-in friendly, and much more. A good ALM tool should help you implement and automate these pillars and components to deliver better business value to your company or organization.

Chapter 3 delves a little deeper into project-management processes and frameworks. It covers some history and also some more modern processes.

Development Processes and Frameworks

Project management is a large part of any ALM process, as you saw in Chapter 2. Therefore it's important to consider which approach best suits your organization.

A project-management process can be a structure imposed on the development of a software product: that is, a way of working that you should follow to successfully deliver an application or a system. You saw in Chapter 1 that the process is an important aspect of successful project completion, so this chapter is devoted to this topic.

Throughout the years, many development processes have come and gone. (If you look closely, they're probably still around somewhere.) They've all tried to improve on the former version or added a new aspect to development. The goal has often been the same, even though the road to that goal has varied. These days, the agile movement has shown good results, as discussed in depth later in this book.

This chapter covers some of the most common project-management methods and frameworks, starting with the oldest and moving on to the more modern, agile, methods. Let's start with one of the best-known project-management models, which has been around since 1970 when it was presented in an article by Winston W. Royce.[1] What is interesting is that Royce actually presented it as an example of a flawed, nonworking model. Obviously, people didn't bother about this fact and started using it as a way to run development projects anyway. The model we're referring to is, of course, the Waterfall model, although Royce didn't call it that.

The Waterfall Model

The *Waterfall model* is a sequential process in which development is seen as a flow steadily moving downward, just like a waterfall, through its different phases (see Figure 3-1).

---

[1]Winston W. Royce, "Managing the Development of Large Software Systems," Proceedings, IEEE WESCON, August 1970, http://www.cs.umd.edu/class/spring2003/cmsc838p/Process/waterfall.pdf.

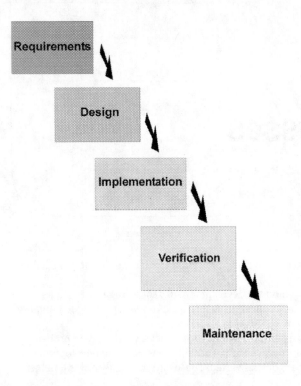

Figure 3-1. *The Waterfall development process*

Royce wrote about seven phases in his original article:

- Requirements specification

- Design

- Construction (a.k.a. implementation)

- Integration

- Testing and debugging (a.k.a. validation)

- Installation

- Maintenance

As shown Figure 3-1, we usually speak of only five of these phases, because the model has evolved over the years. The thought is that the phases are carried out sequentially and you never go back to what has been done. For example, when requirements specifications are finished, they're virtually written in stone. After the spec is written, you move on to the next step—in this case, the design phase—where you model your system and lay out the architecture. This effort can be seen as the blueprint of the system. In this phase, you transform the requirements into a design you can give to the developers to realize into code.

When the blueprint is ready, you can move on to the next step, which is implementation. Now the coders do their magic and the blueprint is transferred into code. At the end of this phase, individual software components are integrated and tested as a system. Different teams of developers may have developed the components, perhaps at different locations, which complicate things as well, because communication tends to be limited in such cases. As you can understand, there is an inherent problem: if you test the system only after development is finished (perhaps 12 months after coding began), you may end up with lots of surprises. Consider the immense rework required if something is found to be wrong at this point. Many months of work may go down the drain, and the project will surely be seen as a failure.

When the implementation phase is done, you move on to testing the software. Hopefully, faults from earlier phases are found and removed in this part of the process. This may be the first time your customers or stakeholders see the final product. If more than a year has passed since the project started, much may have happened to the requirements; and because you can't go back to earlier phases, you may be stuck with requirements that are out of date or wrong. When testing is complete, you install the software and deliver it to maintenance.

It's important to remember that you don't move to the next phase until the previous one is completely finished. There is no jumping back and forth between them, and they can't overlap.

The Waterfall model has been widely accepted and is used a lot—especially in the public sector, such as at the U.S. Department of Defense, NASA, and many other large government projects. This has changed a bit lately (luckily), and more agile methods like Scrum are being implemented at these organizations as well.

The Waterfall method can be great when you know that nothing much will change during your project. Let's say you're about to build a road. After gathering all the requirements for the road, you can assume that they won't change much during the process. The same goes for the blueprints. Sure, some small things may change, such as placement of road signs and streetlights, for instance, but on the whole it's pretty solid after it's approved. When you have such a project, the Waterfall model works very well. Transforming the road example to a development project, a standard product like a finance system may be static after the requirements are set, and the Waterfall model could work well. But even with that kind of development effort, things change. According to Ken Schwaber of the Agile Alliance, and co-father of Scrum, about 35% of all requirements in a project change, which is a very high number and hence introduces risk into the project.

Generally, the earlier you can find bugs, the easier and less expensive they are to fix. Steve McConnell estimates that "a requirements defect that is left undetected until construction or maintenance will cost 50 to 200 times as much to fix as it would have cost to fix at requirements time."[2] This is the reason all phases in the Waterfall model must be 100% complete and absolutely correct before you move on to the next phase. The aim is to catch errors early, to avoid problems and costs in the end.

There are many solid arguments for using the model, at least at first sight. But as you saw in Chapter 1, most development projects are more complex than implementing a standard system. This means it's almost impossible to get one phase perfect before moving on to the next. Just getting all requirements correct is a tremendous task, because the user/stakeholder probably won't be aware of exactly what they want until they have a working prototype to investigate. Then, and only then, can they truly comment on it. It's also then that they get a feeling for what is possible to accomplish with the software. If this awareness occurs late in the project, the changes to requirements are hard to implement.

One cornerstone of software development is documentation. A great deal of focus goes into documenting work. You need design documents, source-code documents, and so on, in order to avoid problems if one of your team members leaves and nobody knows what they were doing. Much knowledge can be lost if you don't have good documentation. If one person departs, it should be relatively easy for their replacement to familiarize himself with the system and quickly become productive.

Another problem that we often run into is that during design, the architect or designers can't know all the difficulties that may arise during implementation. Some features can be hard to build or integrate when you weren't aware of them earlier. How do you handle that if you can't go back to the design and change it after you've left it? Some requirements may also be contradictory, but this may only become apparent during implementation. This will obviously be difficult to solve without changing work done in earlier phases.

Not even Winston Royce really believed in the Waterfall model. Instead, he wrote his paper to explain how to change this model into an iterative one, with feedback from each phase affecting subsequent phases. The strange thing is that this fact has been virtually ignored, and the Waterfall model has been given a huge amount of attention through the years.

---

[2]Steve McConnell, *Rapid Development: Taming Wild Software Schedules* (Microsoft Press, 1996).

Spiral Model

Barry Boehm defined the *Spiral model* in a 1988 article.[3] Although it wasn't the first model to discuss iterative development, Harry Boehm was the first person to explain why iteration matters.

Originally, the iterations were typically six months to two years long. Each phase starts with a design goal and ends with the customer or stakeholder reviewing the progress so far. At each phase of a Spiral project, analysis and engineering efforts are applied, with a focus on the end goal of the project: the business value.

The steps in the Spiral model can be described as follows (see Figure 3-2). Remember, this is a simplified view:

1. The *requirements are defined* in as much detail as possible. Interviews with a number of users representing all the external or internal users and other aspects of the existing system are often used at this stage.

2. A *preliminary design* is created for the new system.

3. Based on the preliminary design, a *first prototype* of the new system is created. Often this is a scaled-down system, showing an approximation of the characteristics of the final product.

4. A *second prototype* is evolved by using a four-step procedure:

    a. Evaluating the first prototype in terms of its strengths, weaknesses, and risks

    b. Defining the requirements of the second prototype

    c. Planning and designing the second prototype

    d. Constructing and testing the second prototype

---

[3]Barry Boehm, "A Spiral Model of Software Development and Enhancement," ACM SIGSOFT *Software Engineering Notes* 11, no. 4 (August 1986).

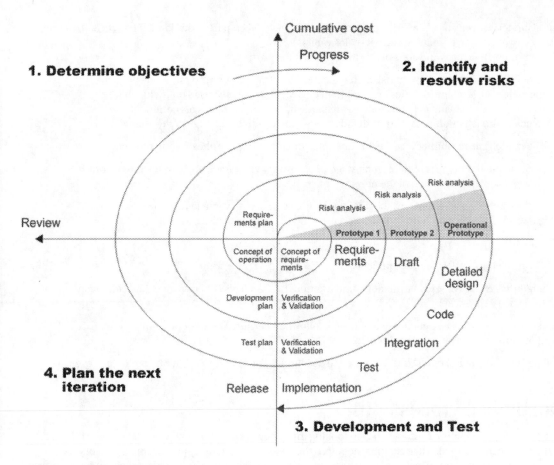

Figure 3-2. *The Spiral model*

If the customer thinks the risks are too great, the project can be aborted. Risk factors can be development cost overruns, miscalculation of operating costs, and any other factor that could, in the customer's judgment, result in a less-than-satisfactory final product.

5. The *existing prototype is evaluated* in the same manner as was the first prototype, and, if necessary, another prototype is developed from it according to the four-step procedure outlined previously.

6. These *steps are iterated* until the stakeholder is satisfied and convinced that the refined prototype represents the final product they wanted.

7. The *final system is constructed,* based on the approved prototype.

8. The *final system is extensively evaluated and tested.* Routine maintenance is carried out on a continuing basis to prevent large-scale failures and to minimize downtime.

The Spiral model is mostly used on larger projects. We have never been part of this kind of project, and neither have any of our co-workers, so it's hard to say if it scales well.

Let's look at some of the pros and cons of this model.[4] First the pros:

- Iterative development helps in risk management. The developers or programmers describe the high-priority characteristics first and then develop a prototype based on them. This prototype is tested, and desired changes are made in the new system. This continual and steady approach minimizes the risk of failure associated with the change in the system.

- The model can accommodates any number of changes during any phase of the project.

- Because the prototype is built in small stages, cost estimation is easy, and the customer gains control over administration of the new system.

- As the model continues toward the final phase, the customer's expertise with the new system grows, enabling smooth development of a product that meets the client's needs.

Now the cons:

- The model works best for large projects.

- It requires extensive skill in evaluating uncertainties or risks. This is a cost driver and can make the expense skyrocket.

- It works on a protocol, which must be strictly followed to ensure smooth operation but sometimes can be difficult to adhere to.

Our feeling is that the Spiral model has decreased in use because agile methods have begun to take over.

Rational Unified Process (RUP)

During the 1980s, a team at Rational Software began looking into a new development model. The *Rational Unified Process (RUP)* was created in 1996, when Rational acquired the Objectory Process by purchasing Objectory AB, which was a subsidiary of Ericsson. The Objectory Process was written by Ivar Jacobson and was instrumental in the development of object-oriented program design.

Rational started this work by going back to the Spiral model and looking into why software projects failed. What was the root cause of such failures in the past? The team also took a good look at which software processes existed at the time and how each of them tried to solve these causes of failure. Some of the reasons for failure were as follows:

- Ad hoc requirements management

- Complexity

- Ambiguous and imprecise communications

- Undetected inconsistencies in requirements, designs, and implementations

- Insufficient testing

- Subjective assessment of project status

- Uncontrolled change propagation

- Poor or insufficient automation

---

[4]For more information, see Amigo G, "Spiral Model Advantages and Disadvantages," November 10, 2010, www.buzzle.com/articles/spiral-model-advantages-and-disadvantages.html; and also Penna Sparrow, "Spiral Model: Advantages and Disadvantages," www.ianswer4u.com/2011/12/spiral-model-advantages-and.html#axzz37EIm4E15.

The people at Rational found that project failure most often was caused by a combination of several symptoms. They also concluded that every project that fails does so in its own unique way. After analyzing their results, the team designed a collection of software best practices, which they named the Rational Unified Process (RUP).

It's important to remember that RUP isn't a single, concrete prescriptive process. It's an adaptable process framework intended to be adjusted by the organization and software team that will use it. The project team should choose the parts of the process that are appropriate for the needs of the specific development task at hand.

The Principles of RUP

The Rational team based their framework on six key principles for business-driven development:[5]

- *Adapt the process*. The project or organization must, as you saw previously, select the parts it needs from the RUP framework. Things to consider here are, for example, how project governance, project size, regulations, and similar issues affect the degree of formality that should be used. There are preconfigured process templates for small, medium, and large projects in RUP so that you can choose more easily. Most companies that we have seen adapt RUP in their own way. One of my former employers had several different RUP adaptations based on different project types.

- *Balance stakeholder priorities*. RUP tries to take a shot at balancing business goals and stakeholder needs between the parties involved, because these often differ and can conflict.

- *Collaborate across teams*. As we (hopefully) all know, software engineering is a team process. A project has various participants, from stakeholders to developers. In Chapter 1, you saw that much development these days doesn't happen at one location, but can be geographically dispersed all over the world. This means collaboration and communication between participants must be good—not only for requirements issues but also for all aspects of the development process. Project status, test results, bug status, release management, design and architecture diagrams, and much more must be on hand for those who need them, when they need them.

- *Demonstrate value iteratively*. One problem with the Waterfall model is that it doesn't allow you to go back if you find things in one phase that throw off things in earlier phases. By working iteratively, you deliver working software in increments. For each iteration, you collect feedback from everyone, including stakeholders, and use this as an input to the next iteration. This way, you can influence the development process and hence the business value while the project is executed. By focusing strongly on iterative development and good risk management, RUP allows projects an iterative risk-assessment process that is intended to ease the effort of delivering a successful project in the end.

- *Elevate the level of abstraction*. By elevating the abstraction level, RUP encourages the use of software patterns, 4GL, frameworks, reusable components, and so on. This approach prevents developers from going directly from the spec to writing their own custom-made code. This also means architecture is discussed at a higher level than before. By using Unified Modeling Language (UML) or built-in features of the development tool in conjunction with higher abstraction, you elevate product architecture to a level at which nontechnical stakeholders can better participate.

---

[5]"Rational Unified Process: Best Practices for Software Development Teams," 1998, www.ibm.com/developerworks/rational/library/content/03July/1000/1251/1251_bestpractices_TP026B.pdf.

- *Focus continuously on quality*. Surprisingly enough, we don't focus enough on quality during many projects. We've had contractors at the Swedish Road Administration that didn't focus on this in their projects. Instead, their primary goal was to suck as much money as possible from the SRA (and from us as taxpayers). This caused problems, as you would guess, because if the SRA didn't keep an eye out, the projects were unsuccessful. RUP encourages continuous quality checks throughout development. Automation of test scenarios, for example, helps you deal with the increasing number of tests arising from the iterative process and the practice of test-driven development (TDD).

The attentive reader (yes, we mean you!) has already noticed that taking the starting letter from each of these principles yields the ABCs of RUP:

- Adapt the process.

- Balance stakeholder priorities.

- Collaborate across teams.

- Demonstrate value iteratively.

- Elevate the level of abstraction.

- Focus continuously on quality.

The RUP Lifecycle

What does the RUP lifecycle look like? It has four major phases (and no, we don't talk about a waterfall here):

- Inception

- Elaboration

- Construction

- Transition

In Figure 3-3, you can see these phases and the effort involved in each on the timeline. A bump early on the timeline for a discipline means the effort is higher at an earlier stage of the project, and vice versa. You can also see that most disciplines stretch over several phases.

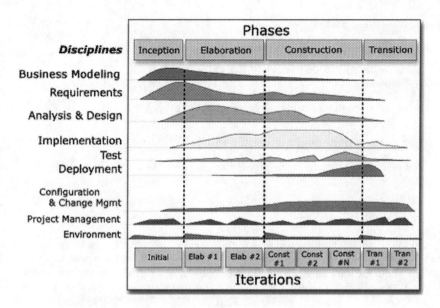

Figure 3-3. *The RUP development process*

Let's look a little closer at these phases.

Inception Phase

As Figure 3-3 shows, the *Inception phase* has a strong focus on business modeling and requirements specifications. The difference from the Waterfall model is that you don't close these topics after the phase has ended. Instead, they're a constant part of all phases throughout the project until its end. This phase establishes a baseline so you can compare actual expenditures to planned expenditures along the way. Before you move on to the next phase, you must pass a milestone called the Lifecycle Objective (see Figure 3-4).

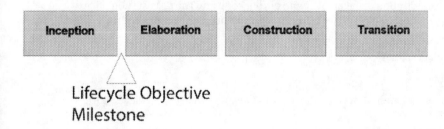

Figure 3-4. *The Lifecycle Objective Milestone*

To pass this milestone, you need to meet these criteria:

- Stakeholder concurrence on scope definition and cost/schedule estimates.

- Agreement that the right set of requirements has been captured and that there is a shared understanding of these requirements.

- Agreement that the cost/schedule estimates, priorities, risks, and development process are appropriate.

- All risks have been identified and a mitigation strategy exists for each.

If you aren't satisfied with the outcome of this milestone or the phase, you can choose to cancel or report this phase for redesign.

Elaboration Phase

During the *Elaboration phase*, you start to see what the project will look like. Figure 3-3 indicates that the analysis and design discipline has its biggest effort here but is required throughout the other phases as well. You also perform other activities in this phase. You start to think about the implementation, how the code will be written, what to code, and so on. Most use cases are developed during elaboration: actors are identified, and the flow of the use case is thought out.

To pass the Lifecycle Architecture Milestone that finishes the Elaboration phase (see Figure 3-5), you should have completed 80% of the identified use cases and turned them into use-case models.

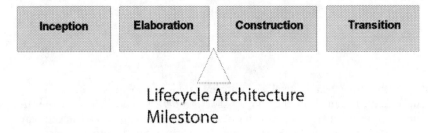

Figure 3-5. *The Lifecycle Architecture Milestone*

You should also have created a description of the architecture of your software. The risk list should have been written, as well as a development plan for the entire project. These are the main criteria for passing the Lifecycle Architecture Milestone:

- Is the vision of the product stable?

- Is the architecture stable?

- Does the executable demonstration show that the major risk elements have been addressed and credibly resolved?

- Is the plan for the Construction phase sufficiently detailed and accurate? Is it backed up with a credible basis of estimates?

- Do all stakeholders agree that the current vision can be achieved if the current plan is executed to develop the complete system, in the context of the current architecture?

- Is the actual resource expenditure versus planned expenditure acceptable?

You must meet a few more criteria before you can pass this milestone, but we don't go into them here. If you can't pass the milestone, you can either cancel or redesign, just as in the preceding phase. When you continue to the next phase, project changes are more difficult to solve if you don't have a model that covers such events.

Construction Phase

Now you're ready for the *Construction phase*. This is where the coding begins and when you implement your architecture. To make sure you catch changes in requirements, you do the development in iterations, each delivering a working prototype. You can show this to stakeholders and end users so they have a chance to provide feedback on it. When you enter this phase, the use cases have been prioritized and divided across the iteration. One good practice is to focus on the highest-risk use cases first, or at least as early as possible, so that you can catch their implications early. To end this phase, you must pass the Initial Operational Capability Milestone (see Figure 3-6) by answering the following questions:

- Is this product release stable and mature enough to be deployed in the user community?

- Are all stakeholders ready for the transition into the user community?

- Are the actual resource expenditures versus planned expenditures still acceptable?

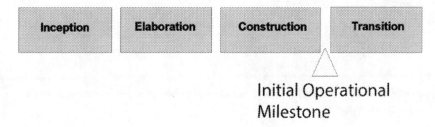

Figure 3-6. *The Initial Operational Capability Milestone*

Transition Phase

When you reach the last phase, the *Transition phase,* you've moved your system/software from the developers to the end users. This phase, as well as the Elaboration and Construction phases, can be performed iteratively. During Transition, you train the end users and the Operations department in their new system. You also do beta testing of the system to make sure you deliver what the end users and stakeholders expect. This means you don't necessarily have the same expectations as when the project started; expectations may have changed during the process. If you don't meet either the end users' expectations or the quality level determined during Inception, you do a new iteration of this phase.

When you've met all objectives, the Product Release Milestone (see Figure 3-7) is reached, and the development cycle ends. The following questions must be answered at this point:

- Is the user satisfied?

- Are the actual resource expenditures versus planned expenditures still acceptable?

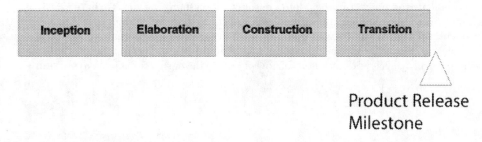

Figure 3-7. *The Product Release Milestone*

Disciplines in RUP

In RUP, we speak of *disciplines*. There are nine disciplines in which you categorize the tasks in a software development project, according to RUP. First are the engineering disciplines:

- Business modeling

- Requirements

- Analysis and design

- Implementation

- Test

- Deployment

Then are three supporting disciplines:

- Configuration and change management

- Project management

- Environment

Let's spend a few moments going over these in more detail. This is interesting especially when you compare this lineup to the description of Scrum later in this chapter.

Business Modeling Discipline

The business modeling discipline is first. The aim of this discipline is to establish a better understanding between business engineering and software engineering. It's a welcome advance compared to the Waterfall approach, because as you've seen, bridging the gap between these two is important. (Chapter 4 gives you an idea of how this can be done.) Business modeling explains how to describe the organization in which the system will be deployed. It also tells you how to use this vision as a basis when outlining the process as well as when selecting roles and responsibilities.

Requirements Discipline

This discipline is responsible for gathering the requirements. It uses these to describe what the system is supposed to do, so developers and stakeholders can agree on what to build.

Analysis and Design Discipline

This discipline takes the requirements and transforms them into a design of the system. The aim is to have a design that can be changed easily when functional requirements change, which of course they will during the project. The design model is an abstraction of what the source code will look like. You can call it a blueprint if you like; it shows components, classes, subsystems, and so on. Having well-defined interfaces between components is another important task for this discipline. It also develops descriptions of how objects in the design collaborate to perform the use cases.

Implementation Discipline

The implementation discipline takes the blueprint and converts it to executable code. Testing of developed components as units also takes place here. Components developed by individual teams are integrated into an executable system by this discipline. The focus is very much on component-based development, which is a way of developing that encourages reuse of existing components. To be honest, this is a good idea in theory, but in real life we've seen very few good examples of component reuse. Most times, *reuse* means a developer using previously built snippets of code instead of components. This discipline makes a good effort to propagate component reuse, but in reality it doesn't seem to be working.

Test Discipline

This discipline has several purposes:

- Verifying interaction between objects
- Verifying all components
- Making sure all defects are fixed, retested, and closed
- Verifying that all requirements have been implemented (correctly)
- Identifying defects
- Making sure defects are addressed
- Making sure defects are addressed before deployment

RUP states that testing should be an integrated part of the entire development project, and we can't agree more. The purpose is to find defects as early as possible, when they can be fixed using minimal effort. Tests are carried out based on four quality dimensions:

- Reliability
- Functionality
- Application performance
- System performance

Deployment Discipline

The activity in the deployment discipline needs to be planned early in the project. Deployment takes place mostly at the end of the Construction phase and the Transition phase; but to successfully deploy an application or system, you need to plan for this event earlier. This discipline focuses on delivering successful product releases. It also focuses on delivering the software to the end users. Included in this work are the tasks of packaging, distributing, and installing the software. Furthermore, the people in this discipline provide help to users so deployment runs smoothly.

Configuration and Change-Management Discipline

RUP distinguishes three areas within the configuration and change management discipline. There is configuration management, which involves the structuring of products. You also need a way to control your releases and the artifacts belonging to them, and these tasks belong to this area. The second area is change-request management, where you keep track of all change proposals you receive for the different versions of the software. The third area is status and measurement management. When a change request is created, it goes through different states in its workflow: it transforms from new, to logged, to approved, to assigned, to completed. This area describes how you can receive reports about the status of the software and its change requests and releases. These reports are important for the project team as well as for stakeholders, so they have a good understanding of the current project status.

Project-Management Discipline

As you've seen in the preceding sections, a project in RUP has two dimensions: the four phases and the iterations within them. The project-management discipline focuses on planning the phases, which is done in the phase plan. You may also need to plan how many iterations (in the iteration plan) and how to handle risks throughout the project. This discipline also monitors the progress of the project.

There are some things RUP doesn't include in the project-management discipline, however. It doesn't cover managing people, which is usually a project-management responsibility. Budget management and contract management also aren't included.

Environment Discipline

The *environment discipline* is the final discipline in RUP. Contrary to what you may think, it doesn't include the software environment. Instead, you it's the environment for the project—that is, the processes and tools you should use when running the project, what work products you should deliver (more about these in a moment), and so on.

Work Products, Roles, and Tasks in RUP

Throughout the project, various deliverables should be produced. RUP called them *artifacts* originally, and that term has stuck in most people's minds. However, after IBM took over RUP responsibilities, the term *work products* was coined, and we use this term from now on.

A *work product* may be an architecture model, the risk list, the iteration plan, and so on. It's a representation of the results of a task. All documents and models produced in the project fall under this heading.

A *task* is a unit of work that provides a meaningful result. A task is assigned to a role. A role in its turn defines a set of related skills, competencies, and responsibilities.

For example, the work-product iteration plan is the result of a task, *produce iteration plan*, which is performed by the role *project manager*. Another example is the task *defining the architecture*, which produces the result, or work product, *architecture model*. This is performed by the role *architect*.

RUP Benefits

Using RUP offers several benefits. Many projects have been completed successfully using an adaptation of this framework, and project quality is significantly improved by using RUP. The problem, however, is that RUP has grown to be an almost impenetrable framework. There is too much to consider and choose from, which makes it very hard to adapt correctly. One of our colleagues said he didn't like a model that required adaptation to that extent. And we can understand that. In addition, the process is too strict and not truly iterative compared to Scrum or any other truly agile methodology. Even Ivar Jacobson, one of RUP's founders, seems to realize that the framework has grown too immense; he has in recent years improved on RUP and created a new, more agile framework.

And agile frameworks is what we focus on for the rest of this chapter. Let's start with the foundation of agile: the Agile Manifesto.

Manifesto for Agile Software Development

In 2001, a group of people met at a Utah ski resort to talk, ski, relax, and try to find common ground for software development. This is the result:

We are uncovering better ways of developing software by doing it and helping others do it. Through this work we have come to value:

- *Individuals and interactions over processes and tools*

- *Working software over comprehensive documentation*

- *Customer collaboration over contract negotiation*

- *Responding to change over following a plan*

That is, while there is value in the items on the right, we value the items on the left more.

Kent Beck	*Ron Jeffries*
Mike Beedle	*Jon Kern*
Arie van Bennekum	*Brian Marick*
Alistair Cockburn	*Robert C. Martin*
Ward Cunningham	*Steve Mellor*
Martin Fowler	*Ken Schwaber*
James Grenning	*Jeff Sutherland*
Jim Highsmith	*Dave Thomas*
Andrew Hunt	

This manifesto is taken from the `agilemanifesto.org` web site and represents the values for a new development approach, and is signed by all the people mentioned. They continue:

On February 11-13, 2001, at The Lodge at Snowbird ski resort in the Wasatch mountains of Utah, seventeen people met to talk, ski, relax, and try to find common ground and of course, to eat. What emerged was the Agile Software Development Manifesto. Representatives from Extreme Programming, SCRUM, DSDM, Adaptive Software Development, Crystal, Feature-Driven Development, Pragmatic Programming, and others sympathetic to the need for an alternative to documentation driven, heavyweight software development processes convened."

These values were the start of a new movement in the software development community, and they have gained a great number of followers since. In addition to its values, the Agile Manifesto lays down the following principles:

- *Our highest priority is to satisfy the customer through early and continuous delivery of valuable software.*

- *Welcome changing requirements, even late in development. Agile processes harness change for the customer's competitive advantage.*

- *Deliver working software frequently, from a couple of weeks to a couple of months, with a preference to the shorter timescale.*

- *Business people and developers must work together daily throughout the project.*

- *Build projects around motivated individuals. Give them the environment and support they need, and trust them to get the job done.*

- *The most efficient and effective method of conveying information to and within a development team is face-to-face conversation.*

- *Working software is the primary measure of progress.*

- *Agile processes promote sustainable development. The sponsors, developers, and users should be able to maintain a constant pace indefinitely.*

- *Continuous attention to technical excellence and good design enhances agility.*

- *Simplicity--the art of maximizing the amount of work not done--is essential.*

- *The best architectures, requirements, and designs emerge from self-organizing teams.*

- *At regular intervals, the team reflects on how to become more effective, then tunes and adjusts its behavior accordingly.*

We believe that most of these values and principles should be present in all software development, but sadly that isn't always the case. Many times, projects we've participated in have delivered a large chunk of software after several months of development. Only then has the customer been brought in to evaluate the work, so both collaboration and incremental delivery have been neglected. Many times the customer has had a lot to say about the result, so we needed to write many change requests to fix the issues or explain why the software worked as it did, and as the customer expected. So, we feel these values and principles are very important and a key concern when we consider our previous projects.

Representatives of various development methods signed the manifesto. Perhaps best known are Extreme Programming (XP) and Scrum, but many of the others are also familiar.

We've chosen to cover XP briefly and Scrum a little more extensively in this chapter. Many of the XP methods are widely used in Scrum projects (and other projects as well). A good example is test-driven development (TDD), which we come back to in Chapter 6. For now, let's start with a short introduction to XP.

Extreme Programming (XP)

Extreme Programming (XP) is a deliberate and disciplined approach to software development. XP, like Scrum, was a direct outcome of the Agile Manifesto and incorporates many of its values. Aspects of these models had been in the minds of their founders for a long time, though, and used in many projects. XP stresses customer satisfaction, an important part of the Agile Manifesto. The methodology is designed to deliver the software the customer needs, when it's needed. XP focuses on responding to changing customer requirements, even late in the lifecycle, so that customer satisfaction (business value) is assured.

XP also emphasizes teamwork. Managers, customers, and developers are all part of a team dedicated to delivering high-quality software. XP implements a simple and effective way to handle teamwork.

- There are four ways XP improves software teamwork:*Communication*: It's essential that XP programmers communicate with their customers and fellow programmers.

- *Simplicity*: The design should be simple and clean.

- *Feedback*: Feedback is supplied by testing the software from the first day of development. Testing is done by writing the unit tests before even writing the code. This is called TDD, and it is becoming a frequently used practice in many projects, not only agile ones. You see later how Team Foundation Server (TFS) implements TDD.

- *Courage*: The software should be delivered to the customers as early as possible, and a goal is to implement changes as suggested. XP stresses that developers should be able to courageously respond to changing requirements and technology based on this foundation.

RUP has use cases, and XP has *user stories*. These serve the same purpose as use cases, but they aren't the same. They're used to create time estimates for the project and also replace bulky requirements documentation. The stakeholders (managers, end users, project sponsors, and so on) are responsible for writing the user stories, which should be about things the system needs to do for them. Stakeholders write stories because they're the ones who know what functionality they need and desire—developers rarely have this kind of information. Each user story consists of about three sentences of text written by the stakeholder in the stakeholder's own terminology, without any of the technical software jargon that a developer may use.

Another important issue is that XP stresses the importance of delivering working software in increments so the customer can give feedback as early as possible. By expecting that this will happen, developers are ready to implement changes.

The last topic we want to highlight with XP is *pair programming*. All code to be included in a production release is created by two people working together at a single computer. This approach increases software quality without impacting time to delivery. Although we've never had the benefit of trying this ourselves, co-workers we've spoken to who have used pair programming are confident that it adds as much functionality as two developers working separately. The difference is that quality is much higher. Laurie Williams of the University of Utah in Salt Lake City has shown that pair programmers are 15% slower than two independent individual programmers, but "error-free" code increases from 70% to 85%.[6] In our opinion, this more than makes up for the decrease in speed.

We can make a reference to my old job as an assistant air-traffic controller here. Many are the times he sat in the tower when airplane traffic was so heavy that he needed help to keep track of every airplane. We're aware that this isn't the same thing, but the fact remains that two pairs of eyes see more than one pair—and this is what makes pair programming so attractive.

To learn more about Extreme Programming, we encourage you to visit `www.extremeprogramming.org/`.

Scrum

Next is one of our favorite development models: Scrum. With all the attention Scrum has been getting in recent years, you may be misled into believing it's a fairly new model. The truth is that the Scrum approach, although not called Scrum at the time, was first presented as "the rugby approach" in 1986. In the January-February 1986 issue of the *Harvard Business Review*, Hirotaka Takeuchi and Ikujiro Nonaka described this approach for the first time.[7] In the article, they argued that small cross-functional teams produced the best results from a historical viewpoint.

It wasn't until 1990, however, that the rugby approach was referred to as *Scrum*. In 1990, Peter DeGrace and Leslie Hulet Stahl[8] highlighted this term from Takeuchi and Nonaka's original article. The term comes from rugby originally where it means the quick, safe, and fair restart of a rugby game after a minor infringement or stoppage. This is also the source of the following quotation:

> *A scrum is formed in the field when eight players from each team, bound together in three rows for each team, close up with their opponents so that the heads of the front rows are interlocked. This creates a tunnel into which a scrum-halt throws in the ball so that front-row players can compete for possession by hooking the ball with either of their feet"*

---

[6]Laurie Williams et al., *Pair Programming Illuminated* (Addison-Wesley, 2003).
[7]Hirotaka Takeuchi and Ikujiro Nonaka, "The New New Product Development Game," *Harvard Business Review*, Jan/Feb 1986, `www.sao.corvallis.or.us/drupal/files/The%20New%20New%20Product%20Development%20Game.pdf`.
[8]Peter DeGrace and Leslie Hulet Stahl, "Wicked Problems, Righteous Solutions," 1990, `http://www.gbv.de/dms/ilmenau/toc/608728446.PDF`.

Keep this definition in mind as we describe the development version of Scrum.

Ken Schwaber started using Scrum at his company in the early 1990s. But to be fair, Jeff Sutherland was the first to call it Scrum.[9] Schwaber and Sutherland teamed up and presented this approach publicly in 1996 at Object-Oriented Programming, Systems, Languages, and Applications (OOPSLA) in Austin, Texas. They collaborated to use their experience and industry best practices to refine the model until it achieved its present look. Schwaber described the model in *Agile Software Development with Scrum* in 2001.[10]

Let's continue bay looking at empirical process control and see what that means in software development.

Empirical Process Control

What is this model, or framework, all about? First, let's define two ways to solve problems. We touched on the issues with projects in Chapter 1. When you have an issue that is similar time after time (like road construction, for example, or implementing a standard system), you pretty much know what to expect from the various tasks at hand. You can then easily use a process—the Waterfall model, perhaps—that produces acceptable-quality output over and over again.[11] This approach is called *defined process control*.

When it comes to a more complex problem, however, like building a software system, you saw earlier that the traditional models don't work. You then must use something called *empirical process control*, according to Schwaber.[12] Empirical process control has three legs to stand on:

- Transparency

- Inspection

- Adaptation

"Transparency means that the aspects of the process that affect the outcome must be visible to those controlling the process."[13] This means to be able to approve the outcome, you must agree on the criteria for the outcome. Two people can't say they're "done" with a task unless they both agree on what the criteria for "done" are.

The next leg is inspection. The process must be inspected as frequently as necessary to find unacceptable variances in it. Because any inspection may lead to a need to make changes to the process itself, you also need to revise the inspections to fit the new process. To accomplish this, you need a skilled inspector who knows what they're inspecting.

The last leg is adaptation. An inspection may lead to a change in the process: this is one example of an adaptation. Another is that you must adapt the material being processed as a result of an inspection. All adaptations must be made as quickly as possible to minimize deviation later.

Schwaber reuses the example of code review when he discusses empirical process control. "The code is reviewed against coding standards and industry best practices. Everyone involved in the review fully and mutually understands these standards and best practices. The code review occurs whenever someone feels that a section of code is complete. The most experienced developers review the code, and their comments and suggestions lead to the developer adjusting his or her code."[14] Simple, isn't it? We could not have said it better ourselves.

---

[9]Jeff Sutherland, "Agile Development: Lessons Learned from the First Scrum," 2004, www.scrumalliance.org/resources/35.
[10]Ken Schwaber and Mike Beedle, *Agile Software Development with Scrum* (Prentice Hall, 2001).
[11]Ken Schwaber, *The Enterprise and Scrum* (Microsoft Press, 2007).
[12]Ibid.
[13]Ibid.
[14]Ibid.

Complexity in Projects

What makes a software development process so complex? We discussed this a little previously, but let's dive deeper here. In theory, building a software system may seem pretty straightforward. You write code that logically instructs the CPU to control the computer. How hard can it be? Alas, it isn't that simple, we're afraid. The people writing the code are complex machines in themselves. They have different backgrounds, IQs, EQs, views, attitudes, and so on. Their personal lives also add to their complexity.

The requirements may also be complex and have a tendency to change over time. According to Schwaber, a large percentage of the requirements gathered at the beginning of a software project change during the project. And 60% of the features you build are rarely or never used in the end. Many times in our projects, several people at the customer site are responsible for the requirements. Often they have diverging agendas as to why and what to build. Often the stakeholders have a hard time expressing what they really want. Only when they see a first prototype of the system do they fully begin to see the possibilities of the software, and only then can they begin to understand what they want.

Rarely is it the case that just one computer is involved in a system, either. Generally there is interaction among several machines. You may have a web farm for your GUI, a cluster for your application tier, a backend SQL Server, some external web services, and often a legacy system, all needing to integrate to solve the needs of the new system.

When complex things interact—as people, requirements, and technology do in a software project—the level of complexity increases greatly. So it's safe to say that we don't have any simple software problems anymore. They're all complex. Schwaber realizes this as well: Figure 3-8 shows his complexity-assessment graph.

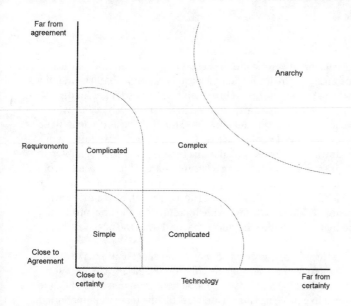

Figure 3-8. *Schwaber's complexity graph*

The projects in the anarchy area are chaotic and unworkable. To get them to their finish lines, you probably need to resolve serious issues before even starting them.

What Scrum tries to do is address this inherent complexity by implementing inspection, adaptation, and visibility, as you previously saw in the section "Empirical Process Control." Scrum does so by having simple practices and rules.

What Scrum Is

Scrum is a powerful, iterative, and incremental process. Many are fooled by its perceived simplicity, but it takes time to master. Figure 3-9 shows the skeleton of the Scrum model, to which we attach the rules and practices. In Scrum, you do development in time-boxed intervals called *Iterations*. An iteration is usually between two and four weeks. Each iteration consists of daily inspections. Such an inspection—or daily scrum, as it's called—is performed by the team once every day at a preset time.

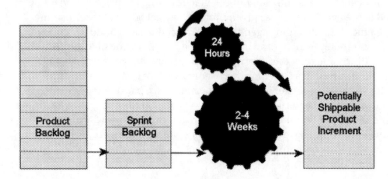

Figure 3-9. *The Scrum skeleton*

During these inspections, team members evaluate each other's work and the activities performed since the last inspection. If necessary adjustments (*adaptations*) are found, they're implemented as quickly as possible. The iterations also conclude with inspections, when more adaptations can be made. This cycle repeats until it's no longer funded.

All the requirements that are known at the beginning of the project are gathered in the product backlog, which is one of the artifacts of Scrum. We come back to this shortly. The project team reviews the backlog and selects which requirements should be included in the first iteration, or *sprint* as it's called in Scrum. These selected requirements are added to the sprint backlog, where they're broken down into more detailed items (*tasks*). Later in the chapter, in Figure 3-13, you can see how many teams visualize their work in a sprint using a Scrum board. This can be electronic, as in the figure, or it can be a whiteboard with sticky notes. The board shows the tasks that have been found for each backlog item and where in the development process each task is currently located (development, test, and so on).

The team then makes its best effort to turn the sprint backlog into a shippable increment of the final product. The team is self-managing, which means members collectively decide who does what and what the best way is to solve problems.

The increment is presented to the stakeholder(s) at the end of the sprint so they can inspect it and make any adaptations necessary to the project. The sprint is most often 30 days, although as mentioned earlier, we often see sprints that last two to four weeks. It depends on the sprint backlog items. When I took his Scrum master certification, Ken Schwaber related that he once had a one-week sprint in a project. The reason was that the team malfunctioned, and this way he could more easily catch the reason and adjust the process so the project ran more smoothly.

The stakeholders' adaptations and feedback are put into the product backlog and prioritized again. Then the team starts the process over and selects the backlog items they think they can finish during the next sprint. These are put into the sprint backlog for the next sprint and broken down into more manageable items. And so it continues, until the stakeholders think they have received the business value they want and funding stops.

If you look again at the three legs of empirical process control, you can see that Scrum covers them nicely. Transparency is implemented by letting the team and stakeholders agree on the expected outcome of the project and of each iteration. Inspection occurs daily and also at the end of each sprint. Adaptations are the direct result of these inspections and a necessary thing in Scrum.

Roles in Scrum

Scrum incorporates different roles. In other models, there are usually many more roles defined in a very strict way, but Scrum has only these three roles:

- The product owner
- The team
- The scrum master

The Product Owner

Let's start with the *product owner*. They're responsible to those funding the project to deliver a product or a system that gives the best return on investment (ROI) they can get from the project. The product owner must acquire the initial funding for the project and make sure it's funded through its lifespan. The product owner represents everyone with a stake in the project and its result. At the beginning of a project, the product owner gathers the initial requirements and puts them into the product backlog. It's the product owner who ultimately decides which requirements have the highest priority based on ROI or business value (for example) and decides into which sprint they should go. During the project, the product owner inspects the project and prioritizes the product backlog and sprint backlogs so that the stakeholders' needs are met.

The Team

The *team* is responsible for development. There are no specific roles on the team. Because the team is cross-functional and self-organizing, it's the members' responsibility to make sure they have the competencies and staff required for solving the problems. It isn't the scrum master who decides who does what and when, as a project manager would do in a traditional approach. These are some of the reasons behind this approach, as taught by Ken Schwaber in his scrum master course:

- People are most productive when they manage themselves.
- People take their commitment more seriously than other people's commitment for them (like when a project manager commits that a person should accomplish something).
- People always do the best they can.
- Under pressure to work harder, developers automatically and increasingly reduce quality.

The team should consist of seven people plus or minus two for optimal results. An optimal *physical team* consists of 2.5 *logical teams*. A logical team consists of one programmer, one tester, a half-time analyst/designer, and a half-time technical writer. The team decides which items in the backlog it can manage for each sprint based on the prioritized backlog.

This thinking is a giant leap from traditional project management and takes some getting used to. Some people don't accept it and find it impossible to work this way.

The Scrum Master

The *scrum master* is responsible for the Scrum process and has to make sure everybody on the team, the product owner, and anyone else involved in the project knows and understands the process. The scrum master makes sure everyone follows the rules and practices of the Scrum process. But the scrum master doesn't manage the team—the team is, as you saw, self-managing.

If a conflict occurs in the team, the scrum master should be the "oil" that helps the team work out its problems smoothly. It's also the scrum master's responsibility to protect the team from the outside world so members can work in peace and quiet during the sprint, focused on delivering business value. The following are the scrum master's responsibilities, again according to Ken Schwaber's course material:

- Removing the barriers between development and the customer so the customer directly drives development

- Teaching the stakeholders how to maximize ROI and meet their objectives through Scrum

- Improving the lives of the development team by facilitating creativity and empowerment

- Improving the productivity of the development team in any way possible

- Improving the engineering practices and tools so each increment of functionality is potentially shippable

The Scrum Process

Now that you know the basics of Scrum, it's time to take a look at what happens during a Scrum project. The product owner, after arranging initial funding for the project, puts together the product backlog by gathering functional as well as nonfunctional requirements. The focus is on turning the product backlog into functionality, and it's prioritized so the requirements giving the greatest business value or having the highest risk come first. Remember that this approach is a value-up paradigm where you set business value first.

■ **Note** *Value up* measures value delivered at each point in time and treats the inputs as variable flows rather than a fixed stock. If you want to learn more about this, see *Software Engineering with Microsoft Visual Studio Team System* by Sam Guckenheimer (Addison Wesley, 2006).

Then the product backlog is divided into suggested releases (if necessary), which should be possible to implement immediately. This means when a release is finished, you should be able to put it into production at once so you can start getting the business value as quickly as possible. You don't have to wait until the entire project is done to begin getting return on your stakeholders' investments.

Because the Scrum process is adaptive, this is just the starting point. The product backlog and the priorities change during the project as business requirements change and also depending on how well the team succeeds in producing functionality. The constant inspections also affect the process.

When a sprint is starting, it initiates with a *sprint planning meeting*. At this meeting, the product owner and the team decide, based on the product owner's prioritization, what will be done during this sprint. The items selected from the product backlog are put into the sprint backlog.

The sprint planning meeting is time-boxed and can't last more than eight hours. The reason for this strict time-box is that the team wants to avoid too much paperwork about what should be done.

The meeting has two parts. The first four hours include the team and the product owner: the latter presents the highest-priority product backlog issues, and the team questions the product owner about those issues so members know what the requirements mean. The next four hours are used by the team to plan the sprint and break down the selected product backlog items into the sprint backlog.

When the project is rolling, each day starts with a 15-minute daily scrum or stand-up meeting (see Figure 3-10). This is the 24-hour inspection. During this meeting, each team member answers three questions:

- What did I do yesterday that helped the Development Team meet the Sprint Goal?

- What will I do today to help the Development Team meet the Sprint Goal?

- Do I see any impediment that prevents me or the Development Team from meeting the Sprint Goal?

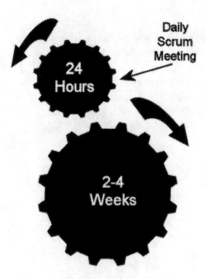

Figure 3-10. *The sprint in Scrum*

The reason for this meeting is to catch problems and hence be able to make timely adjustments to the process. It's the scrum master's responsibility to help team members get rid of any impediments they may have.

When a sprint comes to an end, a *sprint review* is held. This meeting is also time-boxed, but at four hours instead of eight. The product owner and the stakeholders get a chance to see what the team has produced during the sprint and reflect on it. But it's important to remember that this meeting isn't a demonstration: it's a collaborative meeting of the people involved.

Now there is only one meeting left: the *sprint retrospective*. It takes place between the sprint review and the next sprint planning meeting. It's time-boxed at three hours. The scrum master encourages the team to adjust the development process, still within the Scrum process and practices framework boundaries, so that the process can be more effective for the next sprint.

What happens if you have more team members than can fit on a Scrum team (seven plus/minus two people)? What if 90 people are involved in the project? Can Scrum scale to handle this? According to Mike Cohn, in an article on the Scrum Alliance web site,[15] you can use a process called *scrum of scrums*:

> *The scrum of scrums meeting is an important technique in scaling Scrum to large project teams. These meetings allow clusters of teams to discuss their work, focusing especially on areas of overlap and integration. Imagine a perfectly balanced project comprising seven teams each with seven team members. Each of the seven teams would conduct (simultaneously or sequentially) its own daily scrum meeting. Each team would then designate one person to also attend a scrum of scrums meeting. The decision of who to send should belong to the team. Usually the person chosen should be a technical contributor on the team—a programmer, tester, database administrator, designer, and so on—rather than a product owner or ScrumMaster.*

---

[15]Mike Cohn, "Advice on Conducting the Scrum of Scrums Meeting," May 7, 2007, www.scrumalliance.org/articles/46-advice-on-conducting-the-scrum-of-scrums-meeting.

By using this technique, you can scale Scrum infinitely, at least in theory.

Some think that documentation and planning aren't necessary in Scrum. Developers like this idea because they don't want to write documents, whereas stakeholders tremble at the thought. But nothing could be further from the truth. Scrum doesn't say you don't documents or a plan. The contrary is true. Planning, for instance, is done every day, during the daily scrum (see Figure 3-11). Documents should also be written, but you scale away documents that aren't necessary—those that are produced only for the sake of documentation and are almost never read after they're produced. You document what is needed for the system and the project. You document your code, you document traceability, and so on.

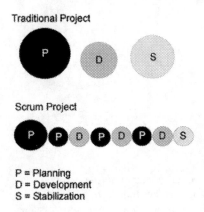

P = Planning
D = Development
S = Stabilization

Figure 3-11. *Planning in Scrum*

That's basically it. Scrum is a lean process and appeals a great deal to us. Joachim had the privilege of doing his scrum master certification during a course held by Ken Schwaber and his product owner certification training at a course held by Mike Cohn; these are two of the legends in the agile world. Unfortunately, some customers and stakeholders find Scrum a bit vague, so they won't try it. They think they have more control with the way they used to run projects and are perhaps afraid to embrace this modern way of doing projects. This hasn't changed over the years, although more and more people we meet have seen what Scrum and agile can do to help them run better projects.

We've found that some companies think they're using Scrum just because they develop iteratively. In many cases, they have changed the Scrum process so that it won't help them solve their development problems—problems that are clearly visible in a true Scrum project. Instead, they use Scrum like makeup to cover the bad spots; and when the project still fails, they argue that Scrum doesn't work, you still don't deliver value, you still have overruns, and so on. When you're implementing Scrum, follow the process and framework, and adjust the organization to Scrum, not the Scrum process to the organization. This can be a real problem in some organizations where, as we said, management resists change and won't use Scrum or agile for the simple reason that they think they will lose control. If you aren't in a position to enforce a new way of working, you need to consider how to most efficiently push management in the agile direction.

The Kanban Method

We'd like to present another method that is usually mentioned with the agile frameworks. *Kanban* is very popular in many organizations and is used by one of our customers today. Even though our preferred project-management method is Scrum for development projects, we realize that Scrum isn't perfect in every situation. Scrum can be scary in the sense that it requires major changes in the way people work in their organizations. It can be hard to implement Scrum fully because humans seem to have an inherent resistance to change. And if you don't have management with you, it's even harder to implement. Wouldn't it be great if you could find a process that was agile but that made it possible for you to make the changes gradually?

Operations can also be difficult to perform using Scrum. Think about this situation for a moment. Let's assume you have three-week sprints for your operations team. One week into a sprint, you suddenly realize that there is a bug in the system that affects production. This bug needs to be fixed right away, so you write a backlog item and present it to the product owner. You need to bring it to the next sprint planning meeting, two weeks from now. Then it will take three weeks for the bug to be fixed, because you have three-week sprints. In the worst case, you'll have to wait five weeks before the fix is available for deployment.

Of course, this is a rare situation. There are obviously ways to handle this better using Scrum. You could, for instance, always have a product backlog item (PBI) of 10% of your available time set aside for bug fixes, and put this PBI at the top of your sprint backlog, allowing you to work on bugs as they're discovered. But we still don't think Scrum is optimal for operations work. This is why we started to look at Kanban.

The name *Kanban* comes from the Japanese word for *signboard*. Kanban goes back to the early days of the Toyota production system. Between 1940 and 1950, Taiichi Ohno developed kanbans to control production between processes and to implement just-in-time (JIT) manufacturing at Toyota manufacturing plants in Japan. The *Kanban method* was developed by David J. Anderson and is an approach to an incremental, evolutionary process as well as systems change for organizations.[16] By using a work-in-progress limited pull system as the core mechanism, it exposes system operation (or process) problems. In such a pull system, tasks that are to be performed are pulled into the workflow, like when you pull a PBI into the sprint backlog. But you can only pull a task into the workflow when there is free capacity to handle the task. It also stimulates collaboration to continuously improving the system.

The Kanban method has three basic principles:[17]

- Start with what you do now.

- Agree to pursue incremental, evolutionary change.

- Respect the current process, roles, responsibilities, and titles.

Let's take a closer look at these.

Start With What You Do Now

The Kanban method doesn't prescribe a specific set of roles or process steps. There is no such thing as the Kanban Software Development Process or the Kanban Project Management Method. The Kanban method starts with the roles and processes you have and stimulates continuous, incremental, and evolutionary changes to your system. This is the thing we like the best about Kanban. It allows you to continue using what you've invested in; the biggest difference is that you can implement big improvements to the existing process without worrying employees.

Agree to Pursue Incremental, Evolutionary Change

The organization (or team) must agree that continuous, incremental and evolutionary change is the way to make system improvements and make them stick. Sweeping changes may seem more effective, but more often than not they fail due to resistance and fear in the organization. The Kanban method encourages continuous, small, incremental and evolutionary changes to your current system.

---

[16]David J. Anderson, *Agile Management for Software Engineering: Applying the Theory of Constraints for Business Results* (Prentice Hall, 2003), and *Kanban: Successful Evolutionary Change for your Technology Business* (Blue Hole Press, 2010).
[17]Taiichi Ohno, Norman Bodek, *Toyota Production System: Beyond Large-Scale Production* (Productivity Press, 1988).

Respect the Current Process, Roles, Responsibilities, and Titles

It's likely that the organization currently has some elements that work acceptably and are worth preserving. You must also seek to drive out fear in order to facilitate future change. By agreeing to respect current roles, responsibilities, and job titles, you eliminate initial fears. This should enable you to gain broader support for your Kanban initiative. Presenting Kanban as compared to an alternative, more sweeping approach that would lead to changes in titles, roles, and responsibilities and perhaps the wholesale removal of certain positions may help individuals realize the benefits of this approach.

The Five Core Properties

David Anderson, in his book *Kanban*, identified five core properties that are part of each successful implementation of the Kanban method:

- Visualize the workflow.
- Limit Work In Progress (WIP).
- Manage flow.
- Make process policies explicit.
- Improve collaboratively.

Let's look at these and see what they mean.

Visualize the Workflow

The knowledge work of today hides its workflow in information systems. In order to understand how work works, so to speak, it's important to visualize the flow of work. The right changes are harder to perform if you don't understand the workflow. One common way to visualize the workflow is by using a wall with cards and columns, called a *Kanban board*. The columns on the card wall represent the different states or steps in the workflow, and the cards the feature/ story/task/result of the workflow, usually referred to as *work items*.

What is great is that you use the steps of your existing workflow—you don't need to enforce a new way of working that dramatically changes the current approach. You basically place the Kanban process on top of what you have, and visualize this flow. This often feels more comfortable to co-workers and makes them more positive about the small changes you're imposing on them.

Figure 3-12 shows the Kanban board that is used to visualize the flow. But wait, some may say: isn't this just like a Scrum board, shown in Figure 3-13? Yes, but there is one significant difference if you compare the figures closely. Above each Kanban board column is a number that identifies the WIP limit. This takes us to the next core property: limit work in progress.

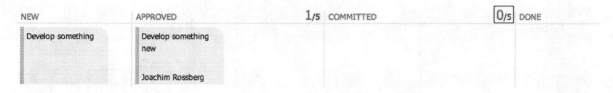

Figure 3-12. *A Kanban board*

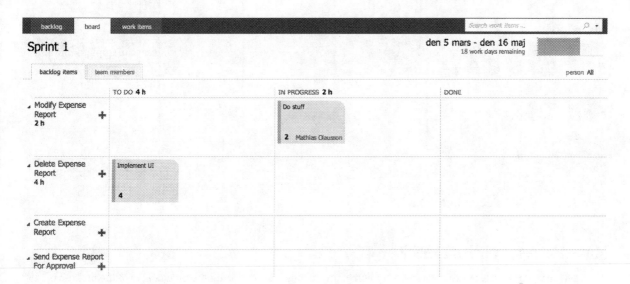

Figure 3-13. *A Scrum board*

Limit Work in Process (WIP)

The WIP limit is important and tells you how many work items you can have in each step (column on the Kanban board). When the limit is reached, you can't pull any new items into this step until a work item leaves the step. Limiting WIP implies that a pull system is implemented on parts or all the workflow. The pull system acts as one of the main stimuli for continuous, incremental, evolutionary changes to your system. It's important, even critical, that WIP is limited at each stage in the workflow.

Manage Flow

The flow of work through each stage in the workflow should be monitored, measured, and reported. By actively managing the flow, the continuous, incremental, and evolutionary changes to the system can be evaluated to determine if they have positive or negative effects on the system.

If a step in your workflow is full, you can't bring any new items into this step. Looking at the board, you can easily see if there is a bottleneck in your flow. If you discover that all columns to the right of the development step on your board are empty, but the development step is full (see Figure 3-14), this means something is stopping development, and people working on development can't finalize their work. You should use idle resources to try to help the developers solve what is stopping them so you can restart the flow and begin pulling new work items into the steps. By having this visibility, you can manage your flow and make sure you handle problems as they arise.

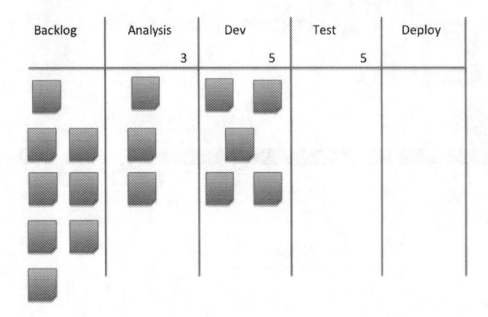

Figure 3-14. *A bottleneck in the flow has been discovered*

Make Process Policies Explicit

It's often hard to improve, or even start a discussion of improving, a process until the mechanism of the process is made explicit. Without an explicit understanding of how things work and how work is actually done, any discussion of problems often seems subjective or emotional. To get a more rational, empirical, and objective discussion of issues, explicit understanding is important. This will most likely lead to consensus around improvement suggestions.

Improve Collaboratively (Using Models and the Scientific Method)

Kanban encourages small, continuous, incremental, and evolutionary changes that stick. David Anderson also discovered this was very effective. Resistance to change, as we've mentioned, is easier to overcome if the steps are small and each step has a great payback. Teams that have a shared understanding of theories about work, workflow, process, and risk are more likely to be able to build a common understanding of a problem and thereby suggest improvement actions that can be agreed on by consensus. The Kanban method proposes a scientific approach to be used to implement continuous, incremental, and evolutionary changes. But the method doesn't prescribe a specific scientific method to use.

Common Models Used to Understand Work in Kanban

Some common models are often used with Kanban to understand how work actually works. We don't go into these in detail here, but we include them for reference:

- The Theory of Constraints (the study of bottlenecks)

- The System of Profound Knowledge (a study of variation and how it affects processes)

- Lean Economic Model (based on the concepts of "waste" [or muda, muri, and mura])

Choosing the Process

Choosing a project-management process can be difficult. Many of the "old" processes have been used for years, and project managers can be very protective of their processes. In many cases they have years and years of experience with those processes; and when something new comes out, resistance to change may blur their vision.

However, IT projects have a tendency to fail in one way or another (see Chapter 1), and many project-management processes weren't intended to be used for projects with the complexity that IT projects often have. That is one of the reasons the agile community came to be. The founders wanted project-management processes that were aimed at software development and not at building roads or houses.

One of the biggest success factors of IT projects during the last decade has, in our opinion, been the introduction of Scrum and its friends. This is confirmed by many of the findings of the Standish Group in its Chaos report (www.standishgroup.com). Using agile methods, you have an opportunity to adapt to the changes that always arise during a project. Instead of working hard on the fixed requirements in a waterfall project and, 18 months after the project starts, realizing that you're building something the business doesn't want, you can now inspect what you've built at the end of each sprint and adapt to the feedback your stakeholders give you. This way, you can steer your project in the right direction as early as possible and deliver real business value.

When we have a choice, we use Scrum during development and Kanban in production. This approach has worked out very well, not only with our company. But sometimes we don't have this choice, because the customer already has processes in place and wants to use them. If we can't convince them to at least try Kanban in these cases, we adjust to the customer and do the best we can. This means we have the challenge of trying to introduce an agile mindset with our customer, hopefully leading to a situation where on the next project, the customer begins to implement some agile methods. This is a little under-cover work, and it can be very stimulating, because it puts the pressure on us to present the ideas in the best way possible. This is also a good way to work if you, in your organization, have resistant managers who refuse to see the agile light.

Keep in mind that the project-management process is a big chunk of the ALM process. A successful project running on a new project-management process can be a big incentive for the organization to keep investing in the ALM process.

According to Forrester, agile adoption has brought about major support for ALM practices.[18] The agile way of working, using frequent inspection and adaption coupled with increased delivery cadence, has made teams more disciplined in their way of working. When agile was introduced, many people thought the opposite would be true, but reality has proven them wrong.

What parts of agile support ALM? Let's take a brief look at what Forrester says and then we will come back to this in more detail in Chapter 4:

- Agile uses a task-based work process. This means that we break down what to do into tasks and work on these.

- The iterative approach to development improves the frequency of your inspection. Instead of waiting for the whole development phase is done we inspect each outcome of an iteration. This improves the feedback loop and together with better visibility for reporting and traceability we have far-reaching implications for ALM.

- Many agile teams use tools that help them collect build and integration information in their continuous integration flow. This enhances visibility and traceability.

- Agile teams often use test-driven development and increase the importance of test artifacts.

- Agile teams plan more frequently than traditional teams. This means they have more information on their projects like estimates, actual results and predictions.

With this we want to stress that ALM sits nicely with an agile approach to project management.

---

[18]Dave West, "The Time Is Right For ALM 2.0+," October 19, 2010, Forrester Research, www.forrester.com/The+Time+Is+Right+For+ALM+20/fulltext/-/E-RES56832?objectid=RES56832.

Summary

This chapter focused on describing some development frameworks you can use for your development processes. Personally we prefere the agile methods best, because they have shown such improvement on project success the last decade. We really think that there are no better way of developing and maintain software right now than the agile methods. If we have a choice we recommend my customers using Scrum for development and Kanban for operations. In this chapter we hope to explain why. Even though we suggest you consider using Scrum or any agile method, we discuss others here as well, so that you can compare and make a decision for yourself.

Choosing the process model is important because it affects the outcome of a project. So before implementing an ALM processes please consider this topic as it's a large part of your ALM implementation. However, remember that in a truly agile manner always be prepared to change and adjust your process, no matter which process you choose. Start with a pilot project and go from there.

■ ■ ■

CHAPTER 4

Introduction to Scrum and Agile Concepts

Chapter 3 looked at different development processes and frameworks. Our experience is that there has been a great deal of improvement in projects over the last few years. To be more specific, we've seen the agile movement make an impact on how projects deliver business value.

The focus of this book, when it comes to processes and frameworks, is on agile methods like Scrum and XP. The reason is simply that agile fits nicely with the concept of ALM, as you saw in Chapter 2.

This chapter looks at how you can use Scrum as an agile project-management model to deliver software. We cover the Scrum process a little more deeply than in Chapter 3, including how you in practice can use Scrum and agile practices such as agile estimation and planning in combination with an ALM tool. This chapter gives you insight into why agile and ALM are a good match.

This chapter doesn't cover eXtreme Programming (XP)—not because it isn't useful, but because XP practices mostly belong to developers, and the focus of this book isn't on development as such. This chapter focuses purely on the project-management features of Scrum.

The Scrum Process

Figure 4-1 shows the Scrum process. The requirements from the business side of an organization are put into a backlog as product backlog items (PBIs). The backlog is an ordered list, with the (currently) most important requirements at the top. When the first sprint starts, the development team, together with the product owner (PO), select a number of PBIs for the sprint backlog (SB) in the sprint planning meeting. The team commits to delivering these sprint backlog items (SBIs) and starts working on them.

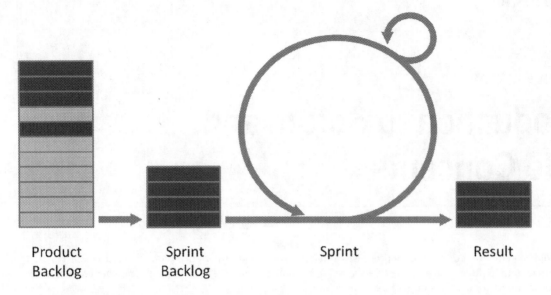

Figure 4-1. *The Scrum process*

A sprint usually lasts 2–4 weeks and is divided into 24-hour increments (working days). Every day, the development team and the SM (SM) meet in a daily scrum meeting to go over the three magic questions:

- What did I do yesterday that helped the Development Team meet the Sprint Goal?

- What will I do today to help the Development Team meet the Sprint Goal?

- Do I see any impediment that prevents me or the Development Team from meeting the Sprint Goal?

The end result of a sprint should be a potentially shippable increment of the software. At the end of each sprint, there are also two meetings:

- *Sprint review*: During this meeting, the team shows the PO (and possibly the stakeholders) what has been done. The PO signs off on the delivery (unless something has not met expectations).

- *Sprint retrospective*: During this meeting, the team assesses what was good, what can be improved, or what needs to be changed for the next sprint.

That's it. No more than that. Seriously. The process is extremely easy to use and learn, although it's difficult to master. But as we said, we've seen great improvements in our customers' projects by taking an agile approach, compared to using a traditional project approach such as Waterfall or Rational Unified Process (RUP).

Let's look at the roles in Scrum and what their responsibilities are. Many of the following sections of this chapter are short and concise. Keep in mind that books and trainings cover these topics, so this book doesn't give you everything. What we aim to do in this part of the book is to exemplify how agile project management can support ALM; and to understand that, you need to know a little more about some important concepts in Scrum.

Roles in Scrum

There are only three roles in Scrum:

- Product owner
- Scrum master
- Development team

Together these three roles create the scrum team. This section of this chapter examines in more detail the responsibilities of these roles when planning and running a Scrum project. Let's start with the product owner (PO).

Product Owner

The PO is the role that most closely equates to a traditional project manager (PM). The truth is that the responsibilities of the PM are divided among all three roles in Scrum, but a significant portion has landed on the PO role. Much of what the PO is responsible for ends up in an ALM toolset—especially at the beginning of the project. Here are a few things the PO is responsible for:

- *What to build, and who should create the vision for the project:* The PO alone decides what the project should build and deliver. The PO has final say in all decisions regarding the "what" question. This isn't always the case, because reality may get in the way, but things are much more difficult if the PO doesn't have the authority to make all decisions.

- *Project delivery:* A PO can never say that the development team didn't build what the PO wanted. If that situation occurs, the PO has done a bad job and probably hasn't been as present and dedicated as they should have been.

- *Requirements and estimation:* When the need for a new system (for example) comes up in the organization, the PO is responsible for gathering and estimating initial requirements. We look at this in more detail later in this chapter.

- *Creating the initial backlog, and continuing to groom it:* Based on the requirements, the PO creates the initial backlog. During the project, the PO is responsible for keeping the backlog in good shape (also known as *backlog grooming*). Included here is the art of breaking down the backlog into manageable pieces, which is something the PO does with the help of the rest of the team.

- *Prioritizing the backlog:* For the team to build the right thing, it's important that the backlog be ordered in some way. By prioritizing the product backlog, the team knows what tasks to take on first. The PO is responsible for this prioritization. The PO probably can't do this alone, so the team is welcome to help and give input.

- *Calculating the estimated budget and ROI:* With initial requirements and estimation done, the PO can calculate the estimated budget and return on investment (ROI) of the project so they can convince stakeholders that the project is necessary.

- *Product management:* The PO should know what and why you build something. All requirements and requests coming in to the project should be filtered through the PO. After looking at the incoming requests, the PO decides what to place on the backlog. Nobody else decides that.

- *Stakeholder management:* The PO is of course not alone with all these responsibilities. The PO needs to manage all stakeholders and end user input so the PO knows what the organization wants; otherwise it's difficult to make decisions. One way of doing this is to schedule repeated stakeholder meetings where the needs and priorities of the organization are discussed.

- *Release management:* It's important early in a project to get an overview of the project releases. Does a specific theme drive a release, or does a certain set of functions equal a release? The PO should make sure this is done early, and then follow up.

- *Team management / staffing the project:* The PO is responsible for staffing the project. Initially, the PO needs experienced people who can help with requirements and initial estimation. These people should then follow the project until it ends, in the best of worlds. Once the project starts, the PO makes sure it's scaled up in the best possible way.

These are just some of the PO's responsibilities. As you can understand, many of these tasks are important for the ALM process in an organization. It's important that the process be able to support the PO and also that the information the PO creates be useful in the process.

Scrum Master

The responsibilities of the scrum master (SM) include the following:

- *Protecting the team:* The team should be able to work without being interrupted by anything. For example, the team shouldn't be disturbed by managers asking members to spend time on other (non-project-related) tasks. If that happens, the SM needs to explain to the manager why the team (or team member) can't do the things the manager asks for. This is essential for the team to deliver what they have committed to deliver.

- *Resolving problems:* If the team or a team member is blocked by an obstacle and can't continue working on a requirement (user story), the SM needs to resolve the problem. The SM needs to clarify what the problem is, why the block happened, and how it can be solved.

- *Making sure the team (including the PO) understands and complies with the Scrum process in the right way:* The SM also needs to make sure the rest of the organization outside the scrum team understands the process and why it's important to stick to it.

The Development Team

Now we come to the team—the people producing the actual code. Here are some responsibilities of the development team:

- *Deciding how to build what the PO has decided to build:* The team is responsible for coming up with the solution, breaking down user stories, giving feedback and suggestions to the PO, and a lot more.

- *Delivering quality code:* The team needs to comply with the requirements in the Definition of Done (DoD), which we discuss later in this chapter.

- *Estimating user stories, both before and during a sprint:* The team needs to estimate the best they can to give input to the PO. Members also need to have a good rapport with the PO so they can point out alternative approaches for the project. If they feel that the PO should make another decision, they're obliged to point that out and argue for a better way.

- *Following the principles of XP:* This may not be in the Scrum guide, but we recommend this from our own experience.

Many of the tasks the development team performs result in information that can be used to determine the project's status. For instance, when updating backlog items, information from the developers is used to create status reports and other reports, providing both visibility and traceability for the project.

Definition of Done

The Definition of Done (DoD) is very important, but it also tends to be forgotten. In many projects, at the end of (or during) a sprint or the project, we've seen arguments between the delivering development organization and the person ordering the project about whether a task has been done. Perhaps testing was not done the way the client assumed it would be, or the software doesn't comply with certain regulations. The following conversation is typical:

> The PO, Sofia, stops by the office of developer Mike to check on how things are going.
>
> S: "Hi. How's the new cool feature you're working on coming along?"
>
> M: "It's going great. I'm done with it right now and will start the next feature soon."
>
> S: "Great! Then I can show it to our customer, who's coming here after lunch. He'll be very excited!"
>
> M: "No, no. Hold on. I am not 'done' done with it. I still need to fix some test cases, do some refactoring, get it into the build process, and so on. I thought you were wondering if I had gotten somewhere with it …"

For the most part, such arguments can be avoided if people sit down together at the beginning and write and sign a DoD.

There are other reasons for having a DoD, as well. In order for the team to estimate a user story, the members need to know when they're done with it. Otherwise, it's very hard to complete the estimate. For a specific user story, you know it's done when you've fulfilled its acceptance criteria. But where do all those general things like style guides, code analysis, build automation, test automation, regulatory compliance, governance, nonfunctional requirements, and so on, fit in? They affect the estimate of a user story as well.

Here is where the DoD comes into play. The DoD tells you what requirements in addition to the user story's acceptance criteria you need to fulfill in order to be done with the story. You include the general requirements in the DoD because they affect all user stories in the end.

The DoD is your primary quality document. If you don't fulfill what is in it, you don't deliver quality. It's essential that the PO and the team agree on the DoD. The DoD is part of the agreement between the team and the PO.

There shouldn't be an argument over this concept during the project. If the PO thinks it's too costly to use pair programming or test-driven development (TDD), have the PO sign the DoD, which specifies that these things have been removed. If, at the end of a sprint, the PO complains about the number of bugs, you can present the document and say that the PO removed essential parts of the testing process, and hence bugs will be present.

A good starting point for a DoD for an approved user story could be something like the following:

- All code is written and checked in (including tests).

- Coding conventions have been fulfilled (these are documented in a separate document and not included here).

- All unit tests have been passed (must be okay before check-in).

- Code is refactored (improved/optimized without change of function).

- All code has been reviewed by at least two people (peer programming or peer review).

- The user story is included in the build (build scripts updated, all new modules included).

- The user story is installable (build scripts updated so the story is included in the automatic install).

- All acceptance tests have been passed:

  - Acceptance criteria must exist.

  - Acceptance tests are implemented (automatic or manual tests).

- The backlog has been updated as follows:

  - All tasks' remaining time is 0.

  - The user story state is Done.

  - Actual Hours has been updated.

  - All tasks are Done.

- The user story has been installed on Demoserver.

- The user story has been reviewed by the PO.

- The user story has been approved by the PO.

- Product documentation has been updated and checked in.

- A user manual has been written.

- The administrative manual has been updated.

- Help texts have been written.

You could also have a DoD like the following for when the sprint is finished:

- All user stories in the sprint fulfill the DoD.

- The product has been versioned (release management/rollback).

- All accepted bugs have been corrected.

- New bugs that have been identified are closed and/or parked.

- 80% code coverage from automated tests is fulfilled.

- All chores are done and approved.

- All integration tests have been passed.

- The sprint retrospective has taken place, and actions for improvements have been identified.

- The sprint review has taken place, with the PO present.

- A performance test of the complete system has been done.

Let's continue by looking at how you can manage requirements and estimations with an agile mindset.

Agile Requirements and Estimation

Agile requirements and estimation is a huge but important topic. This section covers some of the most important topics here, but there are a lot of ways you can manage requirements and estimates. If you want to master this subject, there are several trainings you can take and books to read. A good starting point is to visit www.scrum.org or www.scrumalliance.com and see what they currently suggest.

Most of the agile planning and estimation tips and tricks in this chapter come from the agile community but aren't specific to Scrum. Scrum really doesn't tell you how to do specific things like planning, estimation, and so on. Scrum is the process framework or process method you use for running your agile projects. However, Scrum works very well with the concepts we look at next.

Requirements

In agile projects, you usually represent requirements in something called *user stories*. These can be looked on as fluffy requirements—a bit like use cases. You write user stories like this:

> As a <type of user> I want <some functionality> so I may have <some business value>.

One example could be

As a manager I want my consultants to be able to send in expense reports through the Internet so that you can be more efficient in your expense report process.

Figure 4-2 shows how Microsoft has implemented a user story into the work item type Product Backlog Item in Microsoft Team Foundation Server (TFS). The terminology is a little different from the previous description, but it works.

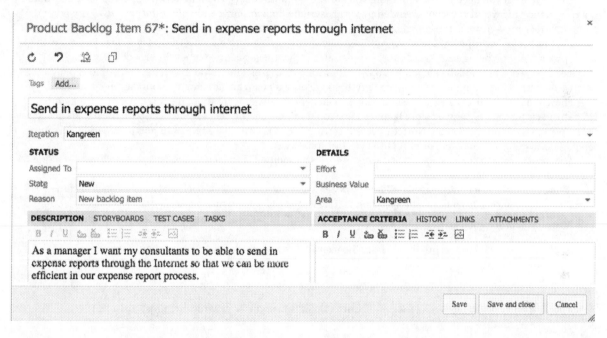

Figure 4-2. *The user story implementation in the Scrum template Microsoft provides with TFS*

User stories capture requirements at a high level and aren't tangled up with detailed functions or implementation details. The details and nonfunctional requirements are instead captured as acceptance criteria for the user story. Based on these acceptance criteria, you can develop acceptance tests at the same time you write the requirements.

The DoD is also important here because it describes other important requirements that all user stories need to fulfill before they're done.

So, how can you begin gathering requirements before you start a project? The PO should use any method they think is suitable. We often use story-writing workshops where important stakeholders, end users, business analysts, experienced developers, and others participate to brainstorm the user stories they can think of. During such a workshop, you focus on the big picture and don't dive into details. These big user stories are often called *epics* because they're large and not broken down yet.

But don't you need to find all requirements at the beginning? No. And that is what makes agile so great. The agile concept builds on the fact that you acknowledge that you don't know and can't know all the requirements early in the project. New requirements and changes to early requirements will pop up throughout the process, and that's okay. The agile approach takes care of this for you. You start with what you have initially, and you continue handling requirements throughout the project. The short version is that you get started right away and are aware that changes and new requirements will come along.

When the initial requirements are finished, you have the embryo of the product backlog. However, before you can prioritize and estimate these user stories, you need to perform a risk assessment so you can get a grip on the risks associated with each and every one of them. A user story with a significant risk associated with it usually takes more effort to finish and should probably be done early in development.

Estimation

To know how much effort is involved with a user story, you need to estimate it. The sum of all initial estimates gives you a (very) rough estimate of how much time the entire project may take. But because you know things usually change over time, you don't consider this estimate written in stone.

You have what you need to do estimation: you know the requirements, you have a DoD, and you have acceptance criteria. In the agile world, it's recommended that you estimate time in something called *story points*. Story points aren't an exact size—instead, they're relative.

Here is an easy example we use when running agile training. Take four animals—let's say a cat, a pig, a zebra, and an elephant. Without being a zoologist, most people can say that the pig is three times the size of the cat, the zebra is twice the size of a pig, and the elephant is maybe four times the size of the zebra. If you have a couple of people sit down and discuss these animal sizes, you can pretty soon come up with an agreement about their relative sizes.

The same goes for user stories. Most developers can agree pretty quickly about the relative size of user stories. User story A is twice as big as user story B, and so on. You don't need to be very experienced with the details of each user story to reach this agreement. Novice developers usually end up with the same estimates as experienced ones. Keep in mind that you aren't talking exact time yet, only relative size.

The most common scale for expressing story points is a modified Fibonacci scale. This scale follows the sequence 1, 2, 3, 5, 8, 13, 20, 40, 100.

Often, teams use a technique called *planning poker* when doing estimates. Each player has a deck of cards containing the numbers from the modified Fibonacci scale. Here is how planning poker goes:

1. The PO/SM reads the first user story.

2. The team members briefly consider the user story and select a card each, without showing it to the others.

3. The team members show their cards at the same time.

4. If the result varies much, the people with the highest and lowest cards explain their reasoning.

5. After a short discussion, the team plays again.

6. When consensus is reached (or the team members are only one step apart), you're finished.

7. If the team still disagrees, you pick the highest value.

But what about time? How do you get down to time? You need to know several things to estimate time. The first is *team capacity*. Consider the following when calculating team capacity:

- How long is the sprint?

- How many working days are available in the sprint?

- How many days does each team member work during the sprint? Consider planned vacation or other days off, planned meetings, and so on.

- Deduct the time for sprint planning, review and retrospective meetings.

The result is the capacity before drag (*drag* is waste time or unknown activities). You should measure drag in each sprint, but at the initial planning it's hard to know how much to include. The longer the project, the more accurate the drag. If you don't know from experience what the drag is, 25% is a good landmark; included in this is 10% backlog grooming.

Now you have the available number of hours in the sprint, and you can connect points and time. You need to know the *team velocity*, which is the number of story points the team can handle in a sprint. Initially this is impossible to know. The easiest way to figure it out is to perform a sprint planning meeting and create a theoretical team velocity. At this meeting, the team breaks down a user story into manageable tasks—and this is where time becomes interesting. During this meeting, the team estimates tasks in hours so they can plan the sprint and decide how many user stories they can take on. The team usually does this as follows:

1. Estimate the first user story in detail.

2. Break down what the team needs to do to deliver the story.

3. Estimate hours for each activity, and summarize.

4. Deduct the summary from the available time the team has in the sprint.

5. Is there still time left?

6. If so, take a new user story and repeat the process until no time is left.

7. Summarize the number of story points from the stories included in the sprint.

Now you have a theoretical velocity.

At this point you can make a rough time plan for the entire (at this point) project. This is good input for the PO in their discussions with stakeholders, and also for ROI calculations.

The sprint planning process continues throughout the project, and the theoretical velocity can soon be replaced with one based on experience.

Backlog

When the initial user stories are in place and estimated with story points, the PO can begin prioritizing the backlog. In Scrum, this is called *ordering the backlog*. Based on the business needs, the PO makes sure the order of the backlog reflects what the business wants. In Figure 4-3, you can see the initial backlog we used to write this book. We did a rough estimate for each backlog item and then did velocity planning. After that, we could see what backlog items should be completed during which sprint (we used two-week sprints).

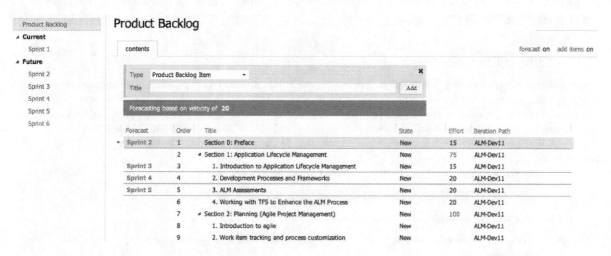

Figure 4-3. The backlog we used to write this book

The PO needs to keep the backlog in good shape throughout the project. This means it needs to be ordered. It also needs fine granularity at the top (perhaps three or four sprints down the list) and rougher granularity further down. Keeping the backlog in your ALM toolset gives you the benefit of visibility and traceability. In the best of all worlds, you can link backlog items to code, check-ins, builds, and so on, giving you good traceability.

The PO can also start to look at release planning at this point. It's important to get an overview of coming releases, especially if you have a larger project. Release planning can be done on the epics (the larger user stories). A good approach is to look for themes among the user stories. What could be useful to release at the same time? If you find such features, you can make a theme from them and plan the theme for a certain release.

When this is done, you can also do a very rough time estimate on the releases—and suddenly you also have a rough time plan for the entire project.

SCALING SCRUM

The PO is responsible for staffing the project. The PO should select an initial team that helps gather and estimate user stories. The team should consist of experienced people (developers, business analysts, and so on) who ultimately should participate in the entire project.

Two to four people on the team may be good during the initial phase, but when the project starts, the team should expand to the number needed (seven plus or minus two people).

If the need arises for more than one team, one or two members of the initial team should participate in the new team. Start small, and expand as needed. We've seen projects start too big and then fail, so don't fall for that.

It's also good if the SM can join the team early.

Now you have as much information as you could possibly ask for this early in a project. The next step is the sprint planning meeting, when the team members (as you saw earlier) select the backlog items they feel they can commit to during the sprint.

During the Sprint

During the sprint, you use several important meetings to inspect and adapt your process. We already covered the sprint planning meeting, which takes place at the start of each sprint. But there are other meetings as well, all important to the agile team.

Daily Stand-Up

The daily stand-up is a meeting that takes place every day during the sprint. This is primarily a developer team meeting and is used to provide status updates to the team members. As the name suggests, this is a stand-up meeting: this comes from the practice of having attendees stand at a meeting because the discomfort of standing for long periods helps keep the meeting short.

The daily stand-ups are kept short, at around 15 minutes, so participants should be reminded that it isn't a working meeting.

As mentioned earlier, all participants should answer these three questions:

- What did I do yesterday that helped the Development Team meet the Sprint Goal?

- What will I do today to help the Development Team meet the Sprint Goal?

- Do I see any impediment that prevents me or the Development Team from meeting the Sprint Goal?

Though it may not be practical to limit all discussion to these three questions, the goal is to stick as closely as possible to them. If further discussions are needed, they should be scheduled for after the meeting. For instance, when team members ask for short clarifications and brief statements, they should try to remember that they should talk about those more after the meeting.

One of the important features of the daily stand-up is that it's intended to be a communication meeting for team members and not a status update for management or other stakeholders. However, it can be valuable for a PO to participate in the meeting so they can catch any issues they need to get involved in. This can remove the need for other status meetings afterward.

The meeting is usually held at the same time and place every working day. All team members are encouraged to attend, but the meetings aren't postponed if some team members aren't present.

This practice also promotes closer working relationships with its frequency, need for follow-up conversations, and short duration, which in turn results in a higher rate of knowledge transfer—a much more active result than a typical status meeting.

Sprint Review

Once the sprint has come to an end, you hold another important meeting: the sprint review. At this meeting, the development team shows the result of what they did during the sprint. They show only the potentially shippable increments of software that they finished during the sprint. Typically this is accomplished using a demo.

Most often the PO, the development team, management, customers, and developers from other projects participate in the sprint review. During the meeting, the project is assessed against the sprint goal determined during the sprint planning meeting. Ideally the team has completed each product backlog item brought into the sprint, but it's more important that the team achieves the overall goal of the sprint.

If some PBIs aren't finished during the sprint, they're put back on the project backlog, and the PO needs to prioritize them for the coming sprint.

Sprint Retrospective

The most important meeting takes place after the sprint review. This meeting is often the last thing that happens in a sprint and is called the sprint retrospective. It's an opportunity for the team to learn from mistakes by inspecting the sprint and adapting to the results of the inspection. No matter how good a scrum team is, there are always opportunities to improve. A good scrum team constantly looks for improvement opportunities, and the team should set aside a brief, dedicated period at the end of each sprint to deliberately reflect on how it's doing and to find ways to improve. Hence the sprint retrospective.

Participants in this meeting should be the development team, the SM, and the PO. Set aside about an hour for this meeting.

There are many ways to do a sprint retrospective. One way is to let the team come up with what was good and what was bad during the sprint. Note these items on a board, and then select (by voting) a number of topics (three to five) from the bad side. Then create action plans for how to improve on them.

Another way is a start-stop-continue meeting. Using this approach, each team member is asked to identify specific things that the team should

- Start doing

- Stop doing

- Continue doing

After an initial list of ideas has been brainstormed, team members proceed as above and create action plans for how to improve on the Stop doing issues. At the end of the sprint, the next retrospective is often begun by reviewing the list of things selected for attention in the prior retrospective.

How Agile Maps to ALM

According to Forrester, agile adoption has brought about significant support for ALM practices.[1] The agile way of working using frequent inspection and adaption coupled with increased delivery cadence has made teams more disciplined in their way of working. When agile was introduced, many people thought the opposite would be true; but reality has proved them wrong.

What parts of agile map to the ALM process? Let's look at what Forrester says.

Agile Captures Task-Based Work

Daily stand-up meetings allow team members to report progress against their tasks. As you've seen in this chapter, the PBIs are broken down into tasks during sprint planning, and each task is reported on, aggregating the results to the original PBI. Using digital tooling for this, such as Mylyn from Tasktop and TFS from Microsoft, allows you to capture effort, time, and other metadata, which can provide valuable insight into the real progress of your software development.

Increased Frequency of Inspection

The iterative approach to development improves the frequency of inspection. During each sprint, you have project inspection at each daily stand-up. At the end of a sprint, during the sprint retrospective, you define what you've done well and what needs to be improved on. This improves the feedback loop and, together with better visibility for reporting and traceability, has far-reaching implications for ALM.

Many Tools Collect Much Information

Many agile teams use tools that help them collect build and integration information in their continuous integration flow. This improves visibility into the build process as well as traceability, because the tools often allow the team to see which requirements, work items, and tests each build included.

▓ **Note** "Continuous Integration is a software development practice where members of a team integrate their work frequently, usually each person integrates at least daily - leading to multiple integrations per day. Each integration is verified by an automated build (including test) to detect integration errors as quickly as possible. Many teams find that this approach leads to significantly reduced integration problems and allows a team to develop cohesive software more rapidly." —Martin Fowler[2]

Test Artifacts Are Important

Agile teams often use test-driven development and increase the importance of test artifacts. Business analysts and quality assurance practices are converging, which is something that agile methods encourage. Agile's emphasis on the definition of *done* and frequent inspection increases the desire to link work items with test plans and cases. The result is that agile teams create simpler requirements but see higher integration with test assets.

---

[1]Dave West, "The Time Is Right For ALM 2.0+," October 19, 2010, Forrester Research, www.forrester.com/The+Time+Is+Right+For+ALM+20/fulltext/-/E-RES56832?objectid=RES56832.
[2]Martin Fowler, "Continuous Integration," May 1 2006, http://martinfowler.com/articles/continuousIntegration.html.

Agile Teams Plan Frequently

Agile teams plan more frequently than traditional teams. Planning takes place when creating work items, during sprint planning, during daily stand-ups, during backlog grooming, and so on.

As a result, agile teams have more information about their projects, such as estimates, actual results, and predictions. This enables ALM to move center stage, because planning activities are an important management component of an ALM application.

Summary

The goal of this chapter has been to show you the details of Scrum so you can understand why the agile approach maps so well to the ALM process. Using agile techniques can help you with visibility, traceability, and collaboration.

The next chapter looks at how you can assess your current status in the organization and find areas where you can benefit from improving your ALM process.

CHAPTER 5

■ ■ ■

ALM Assessments

An *assessment* is an evaluation of, for example, a process. In your work, you may need to perform an assessment of a given situation. Such an assessment is often based on a questionnaire in either digital or analog form. Users answers questions, and a score is calculated based on their answers. It could be describing a system's present architecture and then coming up with a plan for improving it, or it could be assessing how a system scales. When you start working with people instead of technology, the focus of assessments is on a different level: suddenly there is a need to consider human factors and not just technological topics. Before modern ALM tools entered the scene, many organizations conducted surveys of how a department functioned, for instance. Often such assessments were performed by interviewing people from the organizations and thereby getting a picture of the situation.

Interviews are complex and result in a lot of information that you must process afterward. When we do assessments, we generally prepare by writing questions on a form used for the interviews. Any follow-up questions are carefully documented and included in later assessments. This form has become our tool, even though it isn't in an application. Instead, we use a Word document that is updated and printed for each interview.

However, we're a bit reluctant to use only tools. We thought about digitizing the questions into a web application or the like and letting the subjects answer the questions themselves, but we didn't want to abandon the interview part. Tools can help, but they can also hinder, because you can become too dependent on them. Another aspect of using tools for this purpose is that if you let a person answer your questions in, say, a web form, you aren't around to ask follow-up questions. These questions enable you to learn much more than you would if you only looked at the answers to the original bunch of questions.

We started working with Microsoft's TFS a few years back when the product was new. We felt that it was a good foundation for taking control of an ALM process. It lacked (and still does, in some cases) some of the support we wanted, but it was a good start, and nothing else was offered on the Microsoft platform to compete with it. The more we dived into it, the more we started thinking of how we best could evaluate an organization to implement TFS at their site. We realized very quickly that ALM was an important part of an organization's ability to improve its software-development cycle, no matter what platform it used. We soon discovered that TFS was an excellent tool to help our customers, but many more tools started to pop up from vendors like IBM, HP, Atlassian, and so on. We now had tools for visibility, traceability, and automation of high-level processes that fit nicely into the ALM concept.

Microsoft released its ALM assessments on the Web some years ago including the Application Platform Optimization (APO) Model. Microsoft provided its APO Model to help IT organizations understand and adopt a more flexible and agile application platform. This felt like a good start, so we set off to figure out how to best use these tools to help our customers implement an ALM process. Previously, we found that many of our customers used only a fragment of the true potential of TFS (most often the version-control system). If we could show them why they should use more features, they would get much more out of it and at the same time be more successful in running their projects.

Over the years this assessment and the concepts they build on have evolved but what I present here are the fundamentals of the assessments. For each change I have considered what I need to change in my own assessments. Keep in mind that Microsoft can change their assessments and that the current version might be different than what I present here.

One of the main benefits of the Microsoft ALM assessment is that it isn't targeted to Team Foundation Server. It can be used to get a good overview of the current status of the ALM process in any organization, using any ALM toolset. That is also why we use it to assess organizations.

Microsoft's assessment tools were pretty much like web questionnaires, which is why we set to work creating an assessment based on Microsoft's application platform capability assessments, but mixed with an interview part as well. The reason is that a tool can't read between the lines. It can't hear what a person says apart from what is actually answered. It's important to have the capability to ask follow-up questions, and to clarify and discuss where needed.

One great advantage of the Microsoft assessments is that after everything is entered into the tool, the tool can handle much of the data processing automatically. This decreases the labor attached to manual processing the large amount of data an interview gives you. You "only" need to make sure you enter the most realistic values into the system, and that's where the interview part can help you. By using the questions from the online assessment as a form for your interviews, you have a good foundation. Then you can use the results of the interviews, including follow-up questions and observations, to enter data into the assessment form, giving you the capability to reflect on each question and choose the best answer for the organization you're working with.

This chapter describes the foundation of the Microsoft-based assessment and also discuss some variations on it done by a group called the ALM Rangers. You start by looking at the Microsoft Application Platform Optimization (APO) Model and continue with examples of assessment questions in more detail.

Microsoft Application Platform Optimization (APO) Model

APO is part of Microsoft's Dynamic IT initiative, which also includes the Infrastructure Optimization Model and the Business Productivity Infrastructure Model. The Dynamic IT initiative has four primary goals:

- Manage complexity and achieve agility.

- Protect information and control access.

- Advance the business via IT solutions.

- Amplify the impact of your people.

These models are aimed at helping customers better understand their organizations' current IT capabilities and, based on these results, take those capabilities to a higher level of maturity.

This section gives a brief overview of the Infrastructure Optimization Model and the Business Productivity Infrastructure Model before focusing on APO.

Infrastructure Optimization Model

With the Infrastructure Optimization Model, Microsoft focuses on four areas: the desktop infrastructure, the server infrastructure, the remote infrastructure (which covers how to handle remote offices or locations), and virtualization. Based on best practices internal to Microsoft as well as on feedback from customers, Microsoft has provided an approach it says does three things:

- *Control costs* by examining hardware, utilities, and space expenses in the data center to see where you can reduce expenses. Costs also can be controlled or reduced by optimizing deployment testing and training expenses as well as reducing security breaches (in addition to other strategies not covered in this book).

- *Improve service levels.* This can be done, for example, by reducing service interruptions caused by security breaches, having a robust disaster-recovery strategy, and avoiding desktop configuration conflicts.

- *Drive agility.* This includes topics familiar to you by now, such as increasing the ability to adapt to business changes.

Business Productivity Infrastructure Model

Microsoft provides a definition for what optimizing your Business Productivity Infrastructure means (http://en.wikipedia.org/wiki/Infrastructure_optimization). Microsoft defines it as follows:

"The Business Productivity Infrastructure Optimization (IO) model includes a complete set of technologies that helps streamline the management and control of content, data, and processes across all areas of your business. It helps simplify how people work together, makes processes and content management more efficient, and improves the quality of business insight while enabling IT to increase responsiveness and have a strategic impact on the business.

The Business Productivity IO Model defines five capabilities that are required to build a more agile infrastructure":

- *Collaboration*
- *Unified Communications*
- *Enterprise Content Management*
- *Reporting & Analysis*
- *Content Creation*

APO Maturity Levels

Let's now move our focus to the APO Model. Before we explain what this is, let's spend some time with the maturity levels Microsoft has identified for the assessment of the APO Model. There are four optimization levels (see Figure 5-1).

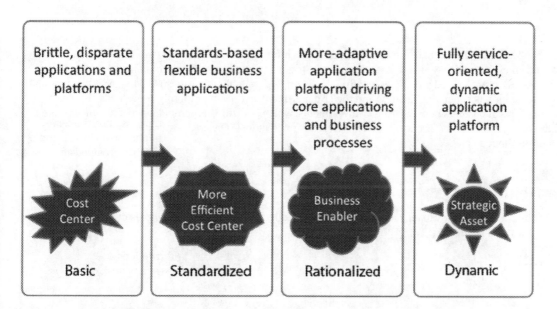

Figure 5-1. *The four optimization levels for categorizing an IT organization (as stated by Microsoft)*

Basic

When a company is classified as a basic organization, it's characterized by brittle, disconnected applications and platforms. This fact hinders rapid adjustments to business changes and also hinders the rapid development and interoperability of business-critical applications. The organization makes no real use of business processes, or these processes (if they exist) are often ill-defined. The processes definitely aren't automated in any way. Such an organization probably has no tool for collaboration between teams and team members, and it definitely lacks the clear connection between IT and business that is crucial for a company to have.

The development process is probably quite rigid, which makes development hard to control. All in all, this leads to higher costs, application backlogs, and lower IT productivity. Management probably views the IT department as just a cost, and its true potential as a strategic asset is clouded by problems.

Standardized

The standardized organization has begun to use industry standards broadly across departments as well as with business partners. These standards could be as simple as starting to use XML, for instance. Furthermore, such an organization has started to take control of its development and data infrastructure, enabling the use of business intelligence reports and analytics. It has also started to automate some of its business processes. The IT department has slowly begun to be seen as a business enabler that can help build more-adaptive systems quickly.

Rationalized (formerly Advanced)

At a rationalized level, IT is truly seen as a business enabler and partner. Now infrastructure and systems are more easily managed throughout their lifecycles. Business processes are well defined and well known. The business side has begun to take advantage of IT and can rely on the IT department to quickly make adjustments when changes in the business occur. Such a company has standardized a robust and flexible application platform for the most critical systems and processes.

Dynamic

A dynamic organization is fully aware of the strategic value of its infrastructure. The organization knows IT can help the business run efficiently and stay ahead of market competitors. Costs are controlled to the company's maximum ability. All processes are automated and integrated into the technology, enabling IT to adjust to business changes and needs. The collaboration between the business and the IT department is working smoothly, as well. It's also possible to measure the effects of business benefits from IT investments, which is a strong argument when showing the value of IT. This kind of organization has also used service-oriented architecture (SOA) to the fullest so that cost-effective systems can be developed.

APO Capabilities

With this background, you're ready to look at the capabilities included in the APO Model. Microsoft defines five capabilities, as shown in Figure 5-2.

APO Capabilities

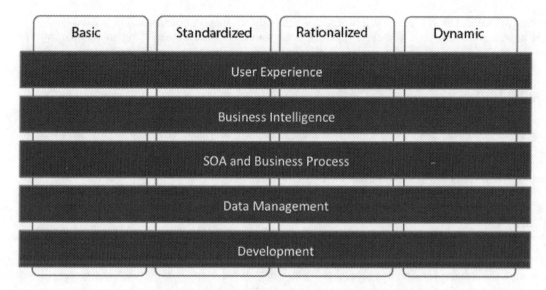

Figure 5-2. *Microsoft has defined five capabilities for its APO Model (http://technet.microsoft.com/en-us/ library/bb821255.aspx)*

User Experience

User experience (UX) is an under-appreciated area. UX is important, but most often this capability isn't included in projects as a special field. Organizations far too often rely on developers to solve UX problems without thinking of the effects bad UX design could have. Not many developers are skilled in this area, and the importance and value of this field are included in this capability. Usability should be a high priority in most cases.

We've seen projects that were considered failures because the user experience was too technical. The developers had a technical view on how to work in the application (or system) and designed it with this as the primary viewpoint. The design was not in line with how the end user really worked, so the user interface required a lot of rework, resulting in higher costs and a delayed project.

Business Intelligence

Microsoft also identifies business intelligence (BI) as a capability. Microsoft and many others have a vision that business insight should be provided to all employees. This leads to faster, more reliable, and more relevant decisions in the organization, because all members of the organization have access to the right information to support good decision making. Areas such as data mining, reporting, data warehousing, data integration, analysis, and more are included here.

SOA and Business Process

SOA and business process is another capability. SOA can be a great thing to implement in your organization, as you may have heard over the years. But SOA in our opinion has cooled off lately, and we don't hear much about it. This capability focuses on the integration between business process management (BPM) and SOA.

This is an immature market, according to some surveys: only around 30% of respondents said they had a combined strategy for SOA and BPM. A significant two-thirds of the organizations had no such strategy, in other words. This might be good for consultants because a market exists that needs help, but it could be disastrous for some companies if they don't change this situation.

Having effective business processes that you're able to quickly adjust to new or changed business needs is essential for an organization these days. You need ways to manage your processes and then automate them in your IT infrastructure. BPM helps manage the processes, and SOA helps implement them in your IT environment.

Data Management

Data management covers what an organization should consider when integrating data-management and -analysis software. How is data storage handled? Will it support business-critical systems reliably? This capability also covers how database development is being carried out, how well the database team is integrated into development projects, and so on. The main focus is to determine how best to build an integrated, well-managed, and always-connected data infrastructure to support your most demanding and mission-critical applications.

Development

Let's look at the development capability. This includes things that can enable an organization to develop applications that connect business processes to meet business needs. It covers areas such as what kind of development platform the organization uses, whether a development process is in place, how the development team and projects are organized, how visibility into the process of a development project is going, and so on.

Application Platform Capability Assessment

Next let's see what an assessment can look like. This assessment was called the Application Platform Capability Assessment, and it existed in three versions:

- Application Lifecycle Management

- Business Intelligence

- SOA and Business Processes

Even though Microsoft has now removed these assessments from their web site they are still a good foundation for our assessments.

We use Application Lifecycle Management in this discussion because it's the most relevant for covering the development process and ALM. It covers all aspects of the ALM process and is very extensive. So in order to get good coverage of the parts of the ALM process you can improve, this is the assessment you should use.

When starting this assessment, you have two options:

- Start Individual Assessment

- Start Team Assessment

In this section we use the team assessment. One big difference compared to the individual assessment, aside from the number of questions and their detail level, is that it's intended to be filled out by more than one person. Microsoft encourages the use of a partner when gathering information about your organization. The best thing about using a partner for such an assignment is that you get an independent view of the answers and the state of the organization.

The ALM team assessment includes many areas; it has eight practice areas, all divided further into various numbers of practices (see Table 5-1). The assessment has about 200 questions (this figure is subject to change), so it covers a great deal of material.

Table 5-1. ALM Practice Areas and Practices

Areas	Practices
Architecture and Design	Architecture framework
	Analysis and design
	Database modeling
Requirements Engineering and User Experience	Elicitation
	Requirements analysis
	Requirements management
	Traceability
	UX research
	UI design and prototyping
	UI implementation
	End-user documentation
Development	Code writing
	Code analysis
	Code reuse
	Code reviews
	Quality metrics
	Database development
Software Configuration Management	Collaborative development
	Database change management
	Version-control repository
	Release management
	Build management
	Change management
Governance	IT governance maturity
	Application portfolio management
	Compliance management

(*continued*)

Table 5-1. (*continued*)

Areas	Practices
Deployment and Operations	Designed for operations
	Deployment
	Environment management
	Operations
	Customer support
	Database deployment
Project Planning and Management	Project initiation
	Project planning
	Project monitoring and control
	Risk management
	Stakeholder management
	Project close
Testing and Quality Assurance	Test resource management
	Test planning
	Test management
	Test types
	Database testing

ALM Rangers' Assessment Guide

There is an alternative to using the Microsoft web-based assessment, which we would like to mention as well. It's from the ALM Rangers,[1] a Microsoft-driven initiative in various ALM areas that has developed an excellent solution you can use in the form of an Excel spreadsheet. The questions are similar to those in the Microsoft web-based assessment, and the practice areas are the same. The difference is that you answer the questions in the spreadsheet and get the result in the same document. For all the latest information on the ALM Rangers' assessment guide, see http://vsaralmassessment.codeplex.com.

As with the Microsoft web-based assessment, one of the biggest advantages with this assessment is that it's platform independent. So if you don't have a Microsoft-based infrastructure, you can still use it with great results. For each of the practice areas, you receive a score on the Basic, Standardized, Advanced, or Dynamic scale (see Figure 5-3).

---

[1] http://aka.ms/vsarunderstand.

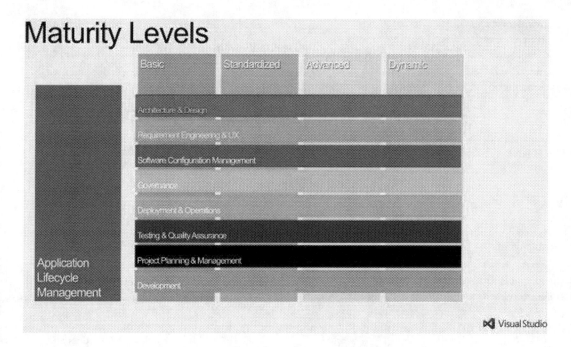

Figure 5-3. The maturity model in the ALM Rangers' assessment (http://vsaralmassessment.codeplex.com)

Let's now take a look at each practice area and the characteristics in more detail, starting with Architecture and Design.

Architecture and Design

Table 5-2 lists the characteristics for each maturity level.

Table 5-2. *Architecture and Design Characteristics*

Basic	Standardized	Rationalized/Advanced	Dynamic
Architecture not properly documented	Architecture role understood and clearly identified, combined with other roles	Dedicated architecture team	Formalized, documented architected process
Inconsistent or nonexistent use of modeling tools	Tools identified, early adoption phase	Architectural tools take into account the deployment process	Consistent inclusion of patterns and practices
No clear process to transform business requirements into technical requirements	Some habits starting to form, some process consistency	Integrated tools used across different teams across different projects	Clearly defined mechanism to share or force usage of patterns and practices across projects and teams
Architecting not considering deployment early in design	Documentation irregularly maintained, not consistent across teams or projects	Leveraging use of practices and processes	Contribution back to the development community internally and externally through the use of published articles, whitepapers and conferences
Unclear understanding of the architect role		Application of practices and processes across teams and projects	

Requirement Engineering and UX

Table 5-3 lists the characteristics for each maturity level.

Table 5-3. *Requirements Engineering and UX Characteristics*

Basic	Standardized	Rationalized/Advanced	Dynamic
Broad assumptions by development team that they know what to build	Consistent quality and format to documented requirements	Multiple types of requirements captured	Institution of Product Change Control Board
Flying by the seat of their pants	Versioning of requirements enabled and tracked	Tracking of requirements relationships and task traceability	Use of impact analysis reports for change requests
Little or no written requirements; no use UX role defined	Requirements accessible to all stakeholders and team members; UX role defined, not necessarily staffed by a UX expert	Use of fully integrated tools for traceability using requirements coverage analysis reports; UX experts involved early in the project	Published metrics on new requirements, requirements implemented, requirements tested, and requirement change requests; UX experts incorporating latest and greatest UI principles
UX done by coders or whoever is available	Some non-integrated tools for UI modeling and prototyping	UI prototyping formally included in development process and integrated with IDE	Continual improvement of UX for subsequent use
No specific tools	Manual customer-review cycle	Use of tooling to support UI modeling templates	UX designers who have a good understanding of technology and limitations
Limited or no customer feedback	User center design principals understood but supported by disconnected tools	Integrated tools to produce UI/requirement/ task matrix	Designers able to understand the intersection of ease of implementation vs. a great-looking UI
Data- or process-driven design	Some consistent user documentation	User-centered design tool (storyboarding) integrated with requirement and task work items	
Gut-feel process, left to developer discretion		User documentation specialists	
No user documentation, or nonstandardized, on- demand, ad hoc user documentation			
Little or no validation with stakeholders			

Software Configuration Management

Table 5-4 lists the characteristics for each maturity level.

Table 5-4. *Software Configuration Management Characteristics*

Basic	Standardized	Rationalized/Advanced	Dynamic
May or may not be using source control	Using non-integrated source-control tools	Use of an IDE integrated source control tool	Highly sophisticated build scripts
Local copies of code	Dedicated build machine	Dedicated configuration management role	Integration of multiple internally and externally produced code modules
Manual on-demand build process	Informal, undocumented build process	Formal, documented build process	Build outcome alerting and monitoring
Build process not documented	Branching and merging understood by lead integrators	Build metrics published regularly	
No traceability between build and content/work performed and requirement	Daily or regular check-ins	Build on demand enabled	
Unclear understanding of branch/merge concepts		Unit tests run after BVT	
Irregular check-ins			

Governance

Table 5-5 lists the characteristics for each maturity level.

Table 5-5. *Governance Characteristics*

Basic	Standardized	Rationalized/Advanced	Dynamic
Projects started with limited justification	Informal certification for chosen compliance program	Formal certification for chosen compliance program	Fully integrated portfolio management tools and process
Projects funded on key influencer opinions	Compliance certification applied and monitored inconsistently across teams.	Using portfolio management techniques, but portfolio- and project-management tools not necessarily integrated	MS Portfolio Manager integrated with project-management system and development system
No ROI evaluation or retrospective	Semi-manual tools and processes (Excel lists, and so on)	Cross-team resources managed, and time assigned	Participation in creation and review process of industry standard compliance programs
No portfolio review process	Random use of initiative targets	Integrated with certification and compliance program	ROI and retrospective supported by metrics
No compliance program or target in place			
No process-improvement initiative in place			

Deployment and Operations

Table 5-6 lists the characteristics for each maturity level.

Table 5-6. *Deployment and Operations Characteristics*

Basic	Standardized	Rationalized/Advanced	Dynamic
Little or no communication between operations and development teams	Stand-alone Help desk incident-tracking tool (training, user issues, infrastructure)	Help desk integrated with bug management	Using Help desk quality metrics on turnaround time, cost of maintenance, and identification of error-prone subsystems
No formal help desk/bug tracking process	Non-integrated bug tracking	Monitored instrumentation hooked into infrastructure and applications	Automated deployment
No tools; e-mail based, manual follow-up	Some monitoring in place	Tools to deploy and validate successful build deployment, smoke tests, testing scripts, and data-generation scripts	Proactive, ongoing monitoring
Infrastructure deployment issues identified and resolved at deployment time	Some procedures and/or approval process in place for build deployment	Approval process with traceability integrated	
No segregated environments, such as development, pre-production, test, UAT, and production	Limited automation and validation of build deployment	Clear cross-functional team identified	
Ad hoc build-promotion schedule	Deployment manager role identified	Infrastructure architecture documented in integrated tools	
Unregulated build promotion	Documented infrastructure	Segregated environments, ownership clearly defined, and promotion procedures well understood and consistent between environments	
Undocumented environment	Segregated environment but ownership unclear		

Testing and Quality Assurance

Table 5-7 lists the characteristics for each maturity level.

Table 5-7. *Testing and Quality Assurance Characteristics*

Basic	Standardized	Rationalized/Advanced	Dynamic
No dedicated Q/A team	Dedicated Q/A group staffed	Organization culture accepting of defined testing policies	Test process improvement group and tools in place
Ad hoc functional testing performed by the development team; closer to debugging than testing	Test plan process defined	Test planning that begins at the requirements phase	Industry leadership on evaluating potential testing tools and strategies
No quality metrics	Un-integrated testing tools in place	Testing measured, and quantifiable process	Defect prevention practiced
Long fix and deploy cycles	Test procedures and environment informally documented	Integrated tools generating publishable metrics	Testing based on statistical sampling, measurement of confidence, trustworthiness, and reliability
High-regression bug rate	Rudimentary progress tracking		

Project Planning and Management

Table 5-8 lists the characteristics for each maturity level.

Table 5-8. *Project Planning and Management Characteristics*

Basic	Standardized	Rationalized/Advanced	Dynamic
No formal stakeholder communication plan in place	Individual, un-integrated, nonstandardized use of project planning tools	Integrated management of bugs, tasks, and change requests	Portfolio management, project management have full integration
Informal or nonexistent processes for estimation, planning, risk management, and scope; gut-feel approach	Tool usage dependent on strength of individual PM	Use of EPM for financial and resource tracking through EPM to VSTS integration	Metrics used to drive projects and aide in estimation and re-estimation
Informal team coordination and task assignment using e-mail, or verbal	Financials manually evaluated by PM	External resources, stakeholders, and partners sharing project information and using integrated tools to perform their role in the project (Sharepoint, Team Plain)	PMO in place
Financials not evaluated by PM on an ongoing basis	PM responsibility clearly assigned	Dedicated PMs	
No clear PM defined responsibility			

Development

Table 5-9 lists the characteristics for each maturity level.

Table 5-9. *Development Characteristics*

Basic	Standardized	Rationalized/Advanced	Dynamic
Developers have up-front knowledge before they start coding regarding the frameworks they will be using	Developers use a framework to support web service devlopment	Developers use a framework to abstract presentation work away from business logic	Developers have mandated training of the latest development technologies
Developers use peer mentoring	Developers have sufficent knowledge of the latest Microsoft technologies to be able to fully utilize the investments in developer tools	Developers use a framework to assist with management of identity	Developers have lead developers with clearly assigned knowledge areas
Doders follow an agreed-on coding standard	Developers use the Security Development Lifecycle	Developers use a state machine engine framework	Developers use code contracts and test-driven development

No matter which way you choose to do your assessment, these characteristics apply. Once you know the score in your area(s) of interest, you can start planning any improvements you need.

Starting the Microsoft Web Assessment

You start the web-based assessment by filling in some information about your company. You can see in Figure 5-4 that you also set a time frame indicating the period in which people can add information to the assessment. You also can fill out the name of the partner you work with during the process.

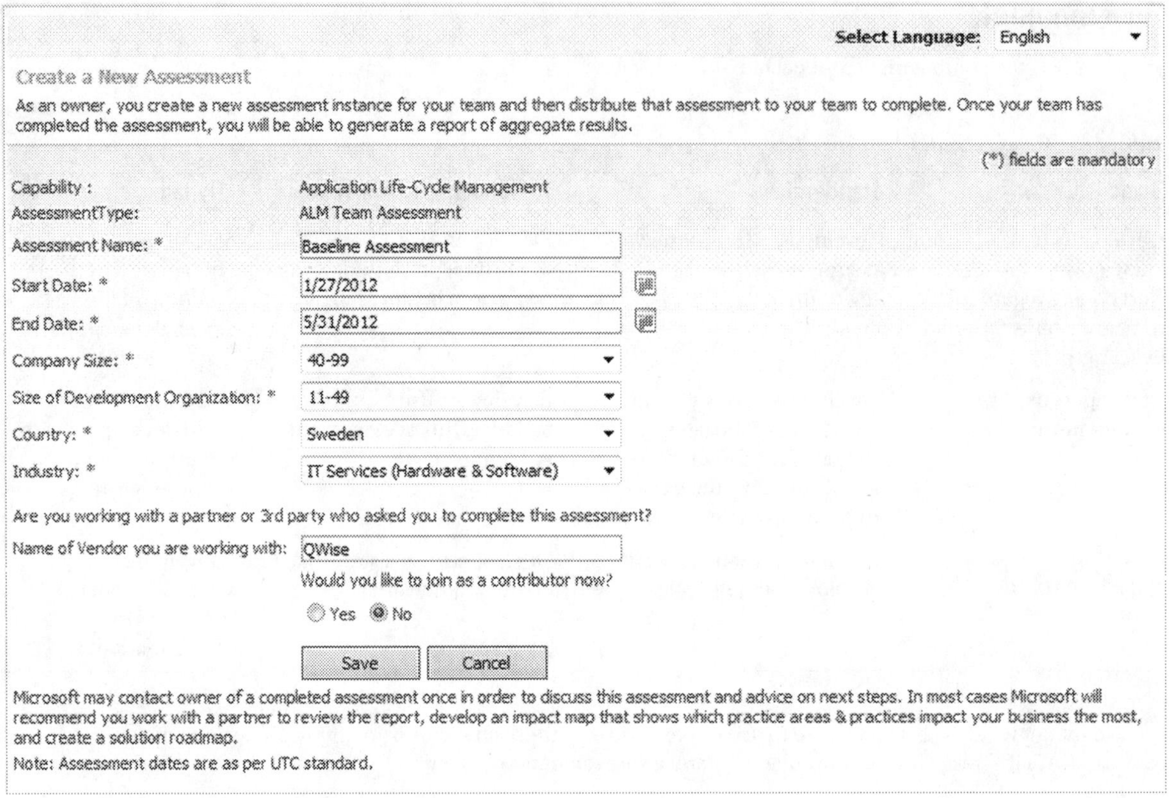

Figure 5-4. *Starting an Application Platform Capability Assessment as an owner*

▓ **Note**   Keep in mind that the GUI may differ after any updates from Microsoft.

The creator, or owner, of the assessment sends an e-mail to all contributors containing the URL of the assessment. Once a participant opens the URL, they're welcomed with a page like the one shown in Figure 5-5.

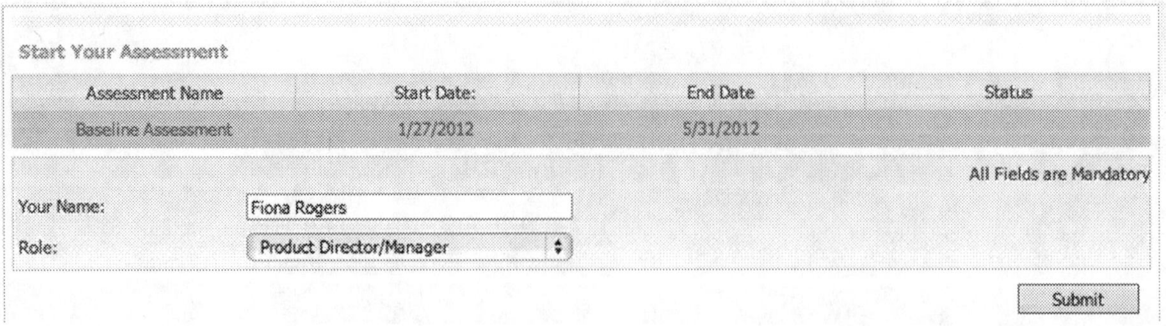

Figure 5-5. *Starting an Application Platform Capability Assessment as a contributor*

When you enter the assessment, there is one page for each of the practice areas. As you know, these areas are divided into practices, and these are displayed as sections on each practice area page. Each section displays the questions for each practice (see Figure 5-6). Some practices have only one question, and others have more, so variance is great.

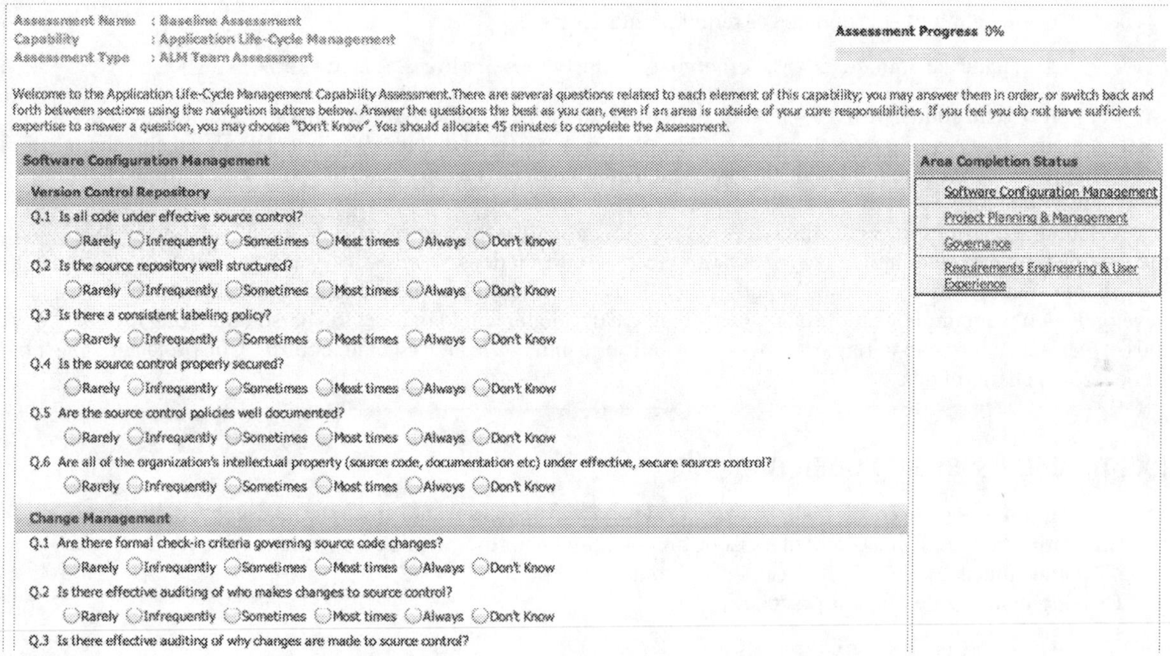

Figure 5-6. Answering an Application Platform Capability Assessment as a contributor

Sample Questions

What kinds of questions can you expect from this assessment? Some are detailed next so you can get an idea of how the practices are examined. Just as you would expect, the questions are more detailed in each area compared to the shorter APO assessment. Let's take a look at two examples.

Example 1: Assessing Requirements Handling

This first example question asks about how you handle requirements in the organization. It tries to find out whether you update the original requirements when changes happen.

Requirements Engineering and User Experience—Requirements Management practice

Q: Are requirements updated as requirements change?

A: 1. Rarely, 2. Infrequently, 3. Sometimes, 4. Most times, 5. Always, 6. Don't know

In many organizations, we have seen requirements remain fixed in the requirements specification no matter what happens to the requirements themselves. What usually happens is that the developers go ahead and change the functionality to reflect the requirement change (which may have come as an e-mail or by phone), without changing the documentation.

Discussing this question at the interview will tell you more than the question itself. Try to find out whether the organization has a requirements system or application, and if it does, whether it's used. You can also ask about how change requests are handled and whether there is a process for that. If the organization has such a process, a developer would not implement the change. Instead, the developer would redirect the person initiating the change to the correct step of the change-request process—usually by sending a formal change request to the project manager or whoever is in charge of this.

Example 2: Assessing Code Analysis

The next example question covers code analysis. Code analysis enables you to make sure developers follow a set of rules indicating how code must be written. Code analysis can include everything from naming conventions to more specific coding practices. This analysis can be automated.

Development—Code Analysis practice

Q: Is there good static code analysis?

A: 1. Rarely, 2. Infrequently, 3. Sometimes, 4. Most times, 5. Always, 6. Don't know

There is no chance of having good code analysis without having it automated in some way. You can use this question to find out more about the company's use of tools for automating the development process. It's a good starting point to dive into this subject, and to see whether the company has other areas where automation is or isn't used. The answers will help you better understand how the organization can benefit from implementing TFS (or any other ALM tool).

Other examples

Other questions and tips on how to use them can be found in the following tables. The first table (Table 5-10) list questions that can be used as a basis for an ALM assessment in the project-management planning phase. These questions are taken from the Microsoft online assessment. Keep in mind that some of these questions are asked based on a Waterfall approach to development. These are useful questions regardless of whether the organization uses an agile method.

Table 5-10 features some input from us. We have chosen not to comment on all the questions but instead focus on some of the most important ones in each area.

Table 5-10. *ALM Assessment Questions for Project Management*

Area	Sample Question	Discussion
IT Governance Maturity	Are IT governance frameworks (such as ITIL, CobiT 4.1, ISO17799) known and applied by the company?	What you want to find out with this question is whether the organization uses a structured IT governance process. If it doesn't, then perhaps you need to look into that in your ALM improvement project.
Application Portfolio Management	Is the customer's business case known, and is it being delivered?	This is important to have. If you're planning an agile process implementation, make sure the product owners are aware of the outcome of any improvement in this area.
	Is there a consistent enterprise directive on how to align the vision of a project to business needs?	This is very important for any successful project. Pay attention to the customer's business needs and see how they can map onto the ALM vision.
	Are any KPIs defined?	A product owner should have this information available for projects.
	Do existing tools roll up into a broader IT portfolio management solution?	If not, suggest using a good toolset solution for this.
Compliance Management	Are compliance requirements identified and tracked by accountable resources in the enterprise?	This is an important question during an ALM assessment and also good input for the development team when it creates its definition of "done" (DoD) together with the product owner. Having a good definition of "done" is essential for all development processes, not just for Scrum.
Requirements Elicitation	Does a "vision" document exist to guide requirements?	Having some kind of vision of projects is always good. Formalizing it by using a vision document might not be necessary. However, it's essential that the team shares the stakeholder's vision.
	Is UML (or similar) used?	Basically you want to get an understanding of how the organization models requirements
	Are tools to standardize the capture and sharing of customer requirements in place?	Suggest that the customer can start using storyboarding, UML, or any other similar technique.
Requirements Analysis	Are modeling techniques used to extract product requirements from customer requirements?	Inquire whether there are modeling techniques in place that could be used to help the organization get started with storyboarding, for instance.
	Are formal user acceptance tests used?	The answer to this affects the definition of "done."
Requirements Management	Are requirements updated as they change?	If not, this is definitely something that most organizations would benefit from.

(continued)

Table 5-10. (*continued*)

Area	Sample Question	Discussion
	Do you capture requirements in an artifact (for example, use case, user story, wireframe, acceptance criteria, and so on)?	If not, the customer needs help gathering requirements. Discuss with them and find out the best way to help them with this.
	Are you able to adjust to the changing requirements of the customer?	If not, this is definitely something that most organizations would benefit from.
	Do you manage requirements using a tool?	If not, help the customer, and suggest using an ALM toolset for this.
Traceability	Is there traceability between requirement and product?	Traceability is a cornerstone in ALM. This is important, so don't let this question slip.
Project Initiation	Does the customer have a project champion or owner, and are they actively involved?	In an agile process, this is important. The product owner needs to always be involved. If the customer doesn't have this, help them realize why this is important.
	Are methodologies and best practices being followed?	Most companies have processes and methodologies, but many times they aren't followed. Discuss, and show the benefits of automating the processes using a tool like TFS.
	Do team members have access to project documents and plans?	Transparency is important and is emphasized in agile communities.
	Is project management based on a formal methodology?	If the organization has no methodology, discuss with the customer and find out what process will benefit them the most.
Project Planning	Is the project plan complete, and does it reflect reality?	Sounds really Waterfall to us. Planning is good, but if the plan doesn't change when reality changes, then what good is it? Discuss, and suggest improvements.
	Is formal resource estimation used?	This is just to understand how the organization plans projects.
	Are the project's vision and scope well defined and understood, and do they map to the business problem?	You want to know if the organization has good collaboration between the business and the IT development side.
	Are project budgets formally approved?	This is just to understand how organization plans projects.
	Is project documentation versioned and archived?	Here, we readily suggest using an ALM toolset like TFS and SharePoint to improve this.
	Are the internal success factors known and understood?	Having success factors and making them known is a good way to increase visibility.

(*continued*)

Table 5-10. (*continued*)

Area	Sample Question	Discussion
Project Monitoring and Control	Is project status tracked against the project schedule?	If you go for an agile approach, discuss the metrics in the ALM toolset, like the burn-down chart and other reports the tooling can help retrieve.
	Are metrics used to manage the project?	Again, this is something a good ALM toolset can help the organization with. Discuss needs, and suggest a way forward using tooling and maybe some custom reports.
	Are all deliverables clearly defined and updated?	An ALM toolset certainly helps with this.
	Are there unexpected changes in personnel?	Aren't there always?
	Do individuals work on several projects concurrently, often switching between them during any given week?	If this is the case, the customer will benefit from assigning individuals to one project at a time. This can sometimes be hard, but context-switching between projects takes its toll on productivity.
	Is status reporting largely automated?	Here is another area where a good ALM toolset will help the customer.
	Is the customer able to make decisions in a timely way?	A development team needs to have answers to questions, and it's essential that the product owner is able to make decisions quickly.
	Is the customer able to provide information in a timely way?	A development team needs to be able to answer questions quickly.
	Are risks known and actively managed?	Risk management is essential. Ad hoc solutions rarely work. So, suggest that the organization use either Scrum, where risks are assessed and mitigated constantly, or another good risk-mitigation strategy.
	Is risk assessment carried out regularly?	Here, you always argue that by using an agile method you manage risk constantly.
Stakeholder Management	Are all the internal stakeholders known when a project starts?	
	Are the external stakeholders known when a project starts?	This is essential to know for any project. Who should be part of stakeholder meetings? If a stakeholder is missing, how can you be sure the project will meet the business needs?
Project Close	Have all the deliverables been formally accepted? Do the outputs match the defined acceptance criteria?	Here is another question where the suggested answer could be to have a good definition of "done" in place. Fulfilling the DoD means the output matches the defined acceptance criteria.
	Has a post-project review been held? Have lessons learned been identified, documented, and shared/published?	Doing a retrospective after a project or after a sprint is a good way to learn how to improve for the next project or sprint.
	Has all the project documentation been archived?	Use a good toolset.

Table 5-11 lists questions that can be used as a basis for an ALM assessment of developer practices. The online assessment has many questions covering this area, but you might want to consider using some of your own as well.

Table 5-11. *ALM Assessment Questions for Developer Practices*

Area	Sample Question	Discussion
Code Writing	Are there standards in place for writing secure code?	This is implemented using a good ALM toolset by adding custom code-analysis rules (or use existing ones).
	Is there a well-defined general coding practice for namespaces, functions, and variable names?	This is implemented using a good ALM toolset by adding custom code-analysis rules (or use existing ones).
Code Analysis	Is there good static code analysis?	If not, a good ALM tool will help the organization with this.
	Is there good performance testing?	If not, a good ALM tool will help the organization with this.
	Is there good stress testing?	If not, a good ALM tool will help the organization with this.
	Are there standards for code coverage of tests?	A good ALM tool will give these statistics for the development team; thus you can use tooling to implement these standards.
Code Reuse	Are patterns and practices established for code reuse?	Code reuse is a good thing. Unfortunately, so far we haven't seen an organization that has succeeded with implementing it in a good way. Ambition is often high, but somehow this never seems to work out.
	Are frameworks used?	Using known frameworks (either your own or publicly available ones) can be a good development practice. This could also belong inside the definition of "done."
	Are code snippets used?	This aims to answer the question: Does the organization use code reuse and knowledge sharing?
Code Reviews	Are effective code reviews carried out?	If not, you can suggest that developers use peer programming, which gives code reviews during code writing.
	Is code often checked in that fails unit tests?	Using automated unit tests and gated check-ins will prevent this.
Quality Metrics	Is there a well-defined and thorough check-in process that includes quality checks?	Here you can definitely use an ALM tool to help. You can set different check-in policies that help you improve quality in most tools.
	Are unit failures measured?	A good ALM tool will give you reports of this.

(*continued*)

Table 5-11. (*continued*)

Area	Sample Question	Discussion
Collaborative Development	Is there an effective versioning and branching strategy?	Most of the following topics are covered by a good version-control system.
	Is there an effective way source can be retrieved for debugging a deployed product?	This is essential for having good traceability.
	Does the source control system allow for development activity at different geographical sites?	In a geographically dispersed organization, this is important.
	Does your source control system support branching, merging, diffing, and labeling?	This is important stuff for traceability and good development practices.
	Do the source repository structure and permissions allow for parallel development?	This is important for understanding how the organization works and what its needs are.
Version Control Repository	Is all code under effective source control?	Most of the following topics are covered by a good version-control system.
	Is the source repository well structured?	This is important for traceability.
	Is there a consistent labeling policy?	This is important for traceability.
	Is the source control properly secured?	Security is always important.
	Are the source control policies well documented?	This is important for visibility.
	Is all of the organization's intellectual property (source code, documentation etc.) under effective, secure source control?	Security is always important.
Change Management	Are there formal check-in criteria governing source code changes?	This is important for traceability and for automating the ALM process.
	Is there effective auditing of who makes changes to source control?	This is important for traceability.
	Is there effective auditing of why changes are made to source control?	In some ALM systems, you can implement a check-in policy that requires comments with a check-in. Sometimes you can also implement a policy that requires an association with a product backlog item.
	Is there effective tracking of builds to source control versioning?	This is important for traceability.

Table 5-12 list questions that can be used as a basis for an ALM assessment in the software testing area.

Table 5-12. *ALM Assessment Questions for Software Testing*

Area	Sample Question	Discussion
Test Resource Management	Is there a dedicated test lead in place?	
	Are there appropriate tools available to perform automated testing?	ALM tools should help with this.
	Is there a management system in place to track work items, defects, and change requests?	Here you have another good opportunity to show the benefits of an ALM tool.
Test Planning	Is a test plan or strategy in place before starting testing?	This is something for the project manager or product owner to consider. You can always benefit from having and executing this plan.
	Is the test team represented at the design review stage?	The test team should always be involved, in our opinion.
	Do test plans consider integration testing with other systems and third-party products?	If you want to automate testing, this is important.
Test Management	Is test execution tracked against the test plan?	If you want to automate testing, this is important.
	Is the test plan followed?	Or is it just a nice paper, never to be seen after finalization?
	Are the appropriate reporting processes in place?	ALM tools should definitely help you getting the metrics you need.
	Are the end-user or customer acceptance criteria well defined and evaluated?	This should be included in the definition of "done."
	Has testing the following nonfunctional requirements been taken into consideration where appropriate: performance, scalability, security, accessibility, regression, localization, and load/stress/soak?	This should be covered by the definition of "done."
	Has code coverage been considered where appropriate?	Discuss with the customer what level of code coverage is necessary. Many tools will help implement the automated tests and give you statistics for code coverage.

(*continued*)

Table 5-12. (*continued*)

Area	Sample Question	Discussion
Test Types	Is user acceptance testing (UAT) used?	Many ALM solutions like TFS includes good tools for handling UAT. The Test Manager in TFS is very helpful here.
	Are automated UI tests performed?	This is easy to implement using, for instance, TFS.
	Are automated integration tests used?	This is easy to implement using, for instance, TFS.
	Are any data-generation tools used?	This is easy to implement using, for instance, TFS.
	Are any stress-test tools used?	This is easy to implement using, for instance, TFS.
	Are any performance-analysis tools used?	This is easy to implement using, for instance, TFS.
Database Testing	Do you have automated testing of your databases?	Don't forget to include database development in your testing.
	Is there suitable test data to ensure that application tests are valid?	This is important for regression testing.
	Do you have a repeatable data set for testing?	You can use a good ALM tool to accomplish this. This is a good developer and testing practice.

Table 5-13 lists questions that can be used as a basis for an ALM assessment in the release-management area. A lot of the assessment questions cover the build process, but many others cover operations and how you deploy applications into production environments.

Table 5-13. ALM Assessment Questions for Release Management

Area	Sample Question	Discussion
Build Management	Is a build process well defined?	This is important for setting up a good automated continuous-deployment strategy.
	Is an automated build-verification process in place?	This is important for setting up a good automated continuous-deployment strategy.
	Is there a library of all successful builds?	You can use a good build tool to help you put the build outcome into specified folders.
	Is there a regular build schedule?	This is important for setting up a good automated continuous-deployment strategy.
	Is the build process automated?	Yes, in many build tools. If the customer lacks this, you can set it up for them.
	Is a build easily reproducible?	Yes, in many build tools. If the customer lacks this, you can set it up for them.
	Can you map source-control changes to specific builds?	Yes, in many build tools. Source-control changes are associated with each build as an associated changeset and can be viewed on the build summary page.
	Is there an effective build failure/success notification process?	Yes, in many build tools. If the customer lacks this, you can set it up for them.
	Is there a build status/progress web page in place?	Yes, in many build tools.
	Are drop locations structured/organized effectively to support DEV/testing/ deployment efforts?	You can tailor it as you want in most build tools.
Designed for Operations	Is an overall architecture in place for the infrastructure environment?	This is important when setting up different development and test environments.
	Do the operations team and development team communicate well at present?	Communication is key to success. Don't forget to involve the infrastructure team.
	Do the developers understand the implications of application deployment to the live environment?	This is important for project success. You don't want to end up with a new application that sinks the production environment.
Database Deployment	Do you deploy database changes to a staging database prior to production?	This is often forgotten. Help the customer if this isn't in place.

This is just a selection of questions you can use to help evaluate the ALM process. Let's now look at how you can use the results of an automated assessment.

Viewing the Results

When all participants have answered their assessments, the assessment owner closes the assessment so that no one can enter any more information. To see the results, the owner clicks the Generate Report button (see Figure 5-7).

Capability	AssessmentType	Assessment Name	Status	Creation Date	Start Date	End Date	Competency Level	Action	Report
Application Life-Cycle Management	ALM Team Assessment	Baseline Assessment	Finished In Progress(0) Completed(3)	1/27/2012	1/27/2012	1/31/2012	-	Modify	🗎

Figure 5-7. *Generating a report for an Application Platform Capability Assessment*

The questions are rated on a five-degree scale (1, 2, 3, 4, and 5), with a sixth choice being the possibility to answer "Don't know." The best score is 5, and the lowest is 1. (This is exactly like the scoring system we had in the Swedish schools a few years ago!)

The system calculates the average score for each capability, for each capability area, and for the entire assessment, and presents them graphically to the user (see Figure 5-8).

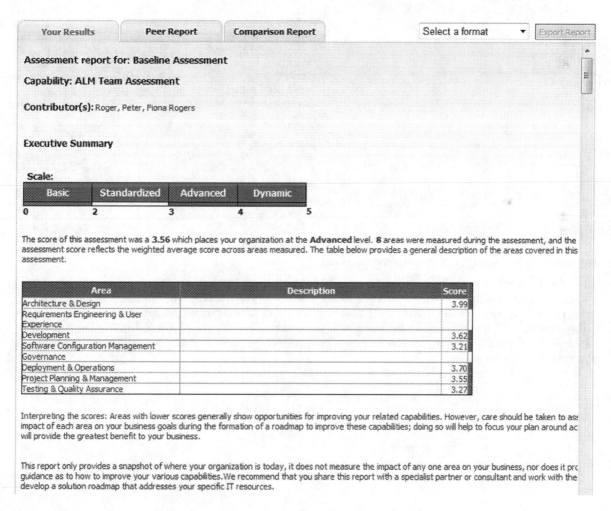

Figure 5-8. *The report for an Application Platform Capability Assessment*

You see a text overview of the entire assessment. The demo here shows a pretty good score of 3.56, which puts this organization at the Advanced level. In the table below the score are the individual practice area scores. You can see the maturity level of each area as well. This information is a useful summary for management to look at. But if you want to see more detailed information, you can scroll down the web page to see the score and maturity level for each practice, as shown in Figure 5-9.

The detailed scores for each area were:

Area	Capability	Score
Architecture & Design		**3.99**
	Architecture Framework	3.88
	Analysis & Design	4.08
	Database Modeling	4.00
Requirements Engineering & User Experience		
	Elicitation	
	Requirements Analysis	
	Requirements Management	
	Traceability	
	UX Research	
	UI Design and Prototyping	
	UI Implementation	
	End-User Documentation	
Development		**3.62**
	Code Writing	3.70
	Code Analysis	3.63
	Code Reuse	3.83
	Code Reviews	3.25
	Quality Metrics	3.83
	Database Development	3.50
Software Configuration Management		**3.21**

Figure 5-9. *Report detail from the score for each practice*

Now you can pinpoint any problem practices, which are practices with lower scores. You can look for the color red or yellow in the right column (not shown in Figure 5-9) to quickly identify such a practice. A manager might want to dive even deeper into the results: farther down is the score for each question (see Figure 5-10). This setup gives you the capability to identify exactly where you have problems, in which practice—and then to use this information to plan corrective measures.

Complete Assessment Report (includes all questions):

Area	Capability	Question	Basic	Standardized	Advanced
Architecture & Design					3.99
	Architecture Framework				3.88
		Architecture definition follows a formal process.			
		There are tools for documenting & sharing Architecture models?			
		Is the architecture well documented?			
		Do major architectural decisions follow a defined process?			3.50
	Analysis & Design				
		Do all team members have access to the design diagrams?			
		Are the diagrams updated throughout the project lifecycle?			
		Are these diagrams stored and version controlled?			
		Is forward/backward engineering performed between the code and the diagrams?			
		If using UML, are Sequence Diagrams created?			
		If using UML, are State Diagrams created?			3.50
	Database Modeling				
		Do you use formal modeling methodologies?			
		Is your Database being documented?			

Figure 5-10. *You can see the score for each question in the assessment*

Microsoft lets you download this report to use it internally. You can save the report in different file formats so that you can process it any way you want.

■ **Note** You don't get any financial information in the Application Platform Capability Assessment report, only maturity scores at different levels of detail.

How to Use the Results

When you assess an organization's ALM process, you need to gather as much information as possible about the client and the client's organization. This is hard work if done manually. We would say it's close to impossible to collect that amount of information from so many people in an organization in a cost-effective way, without using a tool.

We used the questions from Microsoft's assessment tools as a basis for conducting interviews with people from ALM organizations. We gathered people from all areas of the ALM process, making sure both the business side and the IT side were represented. Then we spent 30 to 90 minutes discussing these questions in one-on-one meetings. After conducting all the interviews, we completed the assessment ourselves and used the interview result as a basis for answering the questions. This way, we obtained a pretty realistic view of the organizations and their ALM processes. The results have also been better and have been more accepted by the organizations when we've done it this way as compared to when we had a single person complete an assessment.

There are several ways to use the technique described in this chapter. We've tried it a few ways. Next we offer a few comments about the assessments themselves. Tools are good in most cases. Tools can help you with many tasks and simplify your life greatly—but tools for assessing a complete ALM process? Can that work?

Using the Application Platform Capability Assessment

The team assessment dives down deep. Keep in mind that a tool can't elicit all the nuances that an observer can. You use the Application Platform Capability Assessment questions as a basis for interviews, and make sure you interview people about their special fields only. Architects answer architect questions, project managers answer project-management questions, and so on. This approach has worked very well for us.

We strongly recommend using an external partner for the assessments. It's often easier to look at an organization when there are no strings attached, and no manager to answer to.

Why Do an Assessment?

Why should you spend the time and money doing an ALM assessment? The best reason is that before implementing a good ALM solution, you need to know what the potential pitfalls in the ALM process really are. Every process has room for improvement, and the assessment is a very good way of finding out where improvements are most needed. You need as clear a picture as possible of the organization's maturity level so you can better anticipate what actions are needed for the organization to improve and thus be more effective.

The value of an assessment can be summarized in terms of what it provides. The assessment

- Gives an analysis of the strengths and weaknesses of the current way of working

- Gives a foundation for prioritizing the ALM effort in the company

- Gives input to creating a roadmap for the improvement process

- Gives a baseline for follow-up assessments to measure the impact of an improvement project

An ALM assessment will help your organization understand the current situation and make informed choices on the way to improve the ALM process. Often you may think you know where a problem lies, but before doing a proper analysis, it's hard to say. Making changes to the wrong thing(s) ultimately costs a lot of money—money better spent on correcting the real problem, which in the end could save money.

An ALM process isn't something to implement all at once. It's best done little by little, piece by piece, starting with the lowest-hanging fruit. If you can show the decision makers the improvements of smaller actions, it becomes easier to get them to fund the rest.

One customer we worked with did an assessment. We performed interviews with people from all parts of the organization. Based on the results, we set up a roadmap forward with the focus primarily on the requirements-management processes. We discovered during the assessment that the company had no structured way of working with stakeholders and the development team. The result was that some projects didn't support the business needs, which caused unnecessary strain between stakeholders and the development side.

We set up a good formal process for handling requirements in an agile context. We set up backlog grooming sessions, set up regular stakeholder meetings to support the product owner, and made sure the product owner was clearly visible and aware of their responsibilities. This way, the organization had a clear and well-known process for managing requirements.

After that, we started working on more technical aspects of the assessment. It ended up really well.

Summary

This chapter has discussed the value of doing an assessment of the ALM process before implementing an ALM process-improvement project. The ALM assessments Microsoft offers are good but are best used in collaboration with an external partner carrying out the process in the form of interviews. You can also use the ALM Rangers' assessment guides to perform a great assessment.

Use the assessment as a baseline for evaluating the impact of an improvement project. After a change in your process, you can perform the assessment again and again to measure and make sure you're moving in the right direction.

The coming chapters focus on the ALM cornerstones, starting with visibility.

■ ■ ■

CHAPTER 6

Visibility and Traceability

As you saw in Chapter 2, ALM has several important pillars, and visibility—or transparency—into development efforts is one of them. Another is traceability, which is closely related to visibility. Many managers and stakeholders have limited visibility into the progress of development projects. Traditionally, the visibility they have often comes from steering-group meetings, during which the project manager reviews the current situation. Some would argue that this limitation is good; but as this chapter shows, if you want an effective process, you must ensure visibility.

Other interest groups, such as project members, also have limited visibility into the entire project, despite being part of it. This often comes from the fact that reporting is difficult and may involve a lot of manual work. Daily status reports take too much time and effort to produce, especially when you have information in many repositories.

You've also seen that traceability is an important part of an ALM solution. But what is it? When we talk about traceability in software development, we usually mean the concept of linking requirements (coming from the stakeholders) to code, builds, test cases, and so on. Having traceability means you can support software-development activities like change-impact analysis, compliance verification or traceback of code, regression test selection, and requirements validation.

This chapter discusses what visibility and traceability mean and why they're important. You also learn about a popular development practice called continuous integration and see how such process automation can enhance visibility and traceability in an ALM 2.0+ perspective.

The Importance of Trust and Visibility

Before we move on, we want to tell you a story. The story centers on a 16-year-old girl named Amelie and her father. This particular week, she and her friends had planned a party for the upcoming weekend. One of her friends, Ellen, had the entire house to herself, because her parents were leaving town.

This wasn't going to be a big party, just Amelie, Ellen, and a few friends. They planned to cook some nice food and eat, maybe with some wine if they could get it. Another friend, Emma, was going to bring two of her friends from out of town as well. Amelie had not met them before, but Emma insisted they were cool.

Everything went well. They ate and talked about the usual things—school, boys, and what would happen during the upcoming summer. Amelie really liked the new friends Emma had brought.

After a while, Emma and her friends disappeared out on the porch. Because Amelie wanted some fresh air, she followed them. Then, Linnea, one of the new friends, produced a strange-looking cigarette and lit up. A sweet scent spread across the porch, and Amelie knew what it was even though she had never tried marijuana herself. Linnea looked at Amelie and offered her a try. Amelie was a little taken back. None of her friends had ever tried this before, at least that she knew about. But suddenly she realized that Emma was smoking away as though she had done it many times before. Even though she was curious, Amelie politely said no. Nobody questioned her decision, and she was glad.

When the clock reached 2:00 AM, Amelie decided it was time to go home. Her father had given her money for a taxi, so she called one. She was in bed before 3:00.

The next morning she went to the kitchen, and while she was preparing her breakfast, her father joined her. "Good morning," he said.

"Good morning," she answered. "How was your evening?"

"You know, nothing much happened. We watched a little bit of TV, had some wine, and went to bed early.

"We had a great evening as well" Amelie said. Then she told her father all that had happened, including the events on the porch.

"What?" her father said in a dismayed voice. "They smoked marijuana? Did you try it?"

"No, of course I didn't," she replied.

"But you can't hang around people who do drugs," he continued, even more upset. "Who is this Emma?"

"C'mon dad, chill," Amelie said. "I didn't try it, as I said. They're just like anybody else. A lot of kids smoke."

"But, but ...," he stammered. He was really worried.

"Dad," she continued, "if you are going to freak out like this when I tell you about what happens at our parties, I can't tell you everything in the future. You must trust me; otherwise I'll give you the edited version from now on. Would you like that?"

Amelie's father had no good answer to this. Of course he trusted his daughter. And of course he wanted to know what she did when she was out with her friends. He had always tried to have an open mind. But this? She was right, of course. If he wanted to hear what happened in her life, he needed to show her that he trusted her—that he could handle even things like this, and he wanted to keep his daughter's trust as well so she would feel able to talk to him if she needed to.

Think about this story. The question of trust is important in any relationship. When it comes to running development projects, it's important as well. Consider what would happen if the development team felt that the product owner (PO) didn't trust the team. What would happen if the PO or other stakeholders couldn't handle seeing all that went on in a project? What would happen if they freaked out every time a work item was delayed or had its status blocked? When this happens, you (or the scrum master) must explain what is shown in the graphs or reports that are available so that trust can be reestablished. Even before starting a project, you should have a session with stakeholders to explain all aspects of visibility and the use of the reports if they have never seen these reports before. Trust is something that requires constant work.

If the PO or stakeholders do overreact constantly, it may result in the team producing fake reports showing that everything is OK in the sprint. The team doesn't want the PO to see anything that may cause the PO to disturb the team's work with questions and worries. The truth is, all projects have ups and downs. That's just the way things are. And if the PO (or any stakeholder, for that part) can't handle this, the team doesn't have the time required to finish their work in the sprint.

This isn't a far-fetched scenario. We know people who've been part of projects in which they produced fake reports just to be able to work undisturbed. Such a lack of trust, running both ways, can be disastrous to a project. It must be caught early on, and actions need to be taken. This book doesn't focus on solving these problems, however. We just want to point out that trust is important for a successful project. And if you have flawed transparency you most definitely run into problems.

What Is Visibility?

The short answer is that *visibility* is the ability to measure progress or status against goals. You need to be able to see how you're doing in a project, for instance. Are you on time? Are you on budget? Do you deliver the things you've committed to in the sprint? These questions are important to a lot of people. Managers wants to know how you're doing because they fund the project, team members need to know the status so they can adapt if progress is slow, the PO needs to know what is going on so they can feel assured you're delivering what they want, and so on.

A good way to see the progress of your project is to look at the burndown chart. In Figure 6-1, a sprint burndown chart shows how many hours are left to finish the work in a sprint. You can also see the ideal trend if you want to finish all the work by the end of the sprint. Burndown charts can be produced for releases, projects, and so on, giving you insight into many different aspects of your progress.

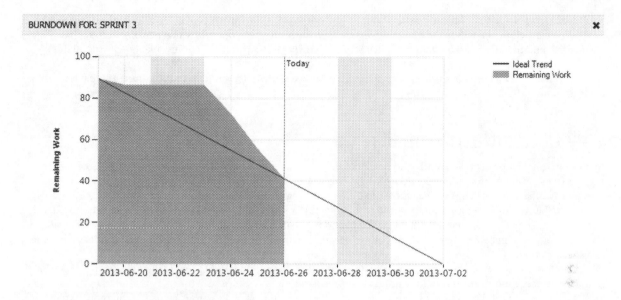

Figure 6-1. *A sprint burndown chart*

Visibility includes other things, as well. To know the current status of your project, it's also important to see how your builds are running. Figure 6-2 shows how build status can be viewed in Microsoft Team Foundation Server. Do you have many broken builds during nightly builds? If so, you might have a problem with the code, or the way the team codes, and need to investigate.

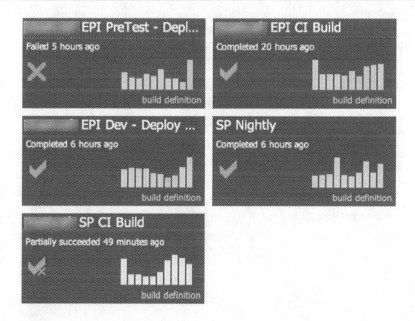

Figure 6-2. *One way of viewing build status in Microsoft Team Foundation Server*

It's also important to be able to see how your tests are going. Do you have lots of failed (automated) regressions tests when a developer checks in code? Seeing this quickly allows the developer to avoid checking in code that will fail the automated build. They can then take action to correct the code and check in code that passes all the regression testing.

Of course, other aspects of software-development processes enhance visibility as well, but we'll stop with these for now.

Why Do You Need Visibility?

In order to run your projects efficiently and deliver high quality, it's essential that you have insight into how they're doing so you can catch problems and make changes as quickly as possible. If a project needs to change course, everyone involved needs to be aware of the issue(s) you're facing.

To do this, you need information regarding the project status to be available to everyone. You can accomplish this by centralizing the information. That way, you can more easily integrate all your processes. For instance, you can integrate your version control system with your project-management tool so that you can see what changes correlate to a specific iteration.

A central repository for information also ensures that the information is consistent in all tools that use it. It's be easier to produce reports and easier to maintain the information.

Having global visibility can help you reroute a ship that's traveling on a disastrous course. It can then help your development team change course when they need to.

An Agile Approach to Visibility

Many agile approaches encourage you to increase your focus on build and release practices. This focus greatly increases visibility into project progress as well as traceability (which is covered in more detail in Chapter 7).

Generally, agile teams plan more frequently than traditional projects. This gives the agile teams more information about their projects, covering everything from high- and low-level estimates to actual results and predictions. Having this information available allows you to get much better visibility into how your projects are doing.

Information in an agile environment is viewed more often, and scrum teams need to see this information on a daily basis in order to change course if necessary. Visibility in an agile environment allows teams to use information in their stand-ups, sprint reviews, demos, and retrospectives.

One of the most popular agile practices is *continuous integration*. This is a good practice that significantly increases visibility into the progress of projects. Let's look at this process in more detail so that you can understand why it's a good practice for providing visibility.

Continuous Integration

> *Continuous Integration is a software development practice where members of a team integrate their work frequently; usually each person integrates at least daily – leading to multiple integrations per day.*

—Martin Fowler

Continuous integration (CI) was introduced by Martin Fowler and is now the de facto standard in agile projects. Once you've worked on a project with a CI process in place, it's hard to imagine how a project could work without it. It can, of course; but an agile project requires new ways of working, and just as Scrum is said to be all about common sense, so is CI. But there are several problems with agile development from a deployment perspective, such as the following:

- *Testing*: As you've seen in earlier chapters, agile projects require that you do testing earlier and more often because software is built incrementally in short iterations.

- *Cross-functional teams*: Ideally, the team should be self-organized, meaning more people need to be able to deploy software.

- *Shippable product in every iteration*: Manual routines used to work, but now it isn't OK to spend a week on installation tasks if the sprint is two weeks.

CI can help to resolve these issues. In fact, Scrum has a solution: use the retrospective to find ways to improve. The next section look at how you can get going with improvements.

Why Should You Implement Continuous Integration?

It can be hard to justify the work to implement CI. Instead of just relying on a gut feeling that this is a good practice and worth the time required to set it up, you can refer to some of our favorite reasons to use CI. It will

- Improve project visibility

- Reduce risks

- Reduce manual routines

- Create shippable software

- Improve confidence in the product

- Identify deficiencies early

- Reduce time spent on manual tasks

Even with these good arguments for why CI makes sense, we occasionally hear concerns like the following:

- *Maintenance overhead*: You need to maintain the build environment and the CI solution. It's hard to argue against this. But show us any factory that works without maintenance—why should a software factory be any different?

- *Effort to introduce*: Sure, it takes some time to get the process started. Not as much for a new project, but for an existing solution you may need to add CI capabilities incrementally to achieve a good return on investment.

- *Quality of the current solution*: Some may argue that the current process is too poor to automate. If you ever hear that argument, make sure you get CI in place.

- *Increased cost*: New hardware must be purchased for the build infrastructure. But think about the savings from raising quality and identifying problems much earlier in the process.

- *Duplicate work*: With CI, you need to automate what you already do manually. Well, yes, initially you do; but the goal should be to share as much as possible of the work that developers and testers do anyway. For instance, the build system can use the same solution files the developer use locally, and developers can use the deployment script to update the local machine when a new version needs to be installed locally.

Finally, to get CI working, the team needs to agree on the rules around the process. If the rules aren't followed, there is a potential risk that the quality of the result will degrade and people will lose confidence in the process. We recommend using the following rules as a starting point:

- *Check in often*: The CI process needs changes in order to work. The smaller the changes you can commit, and the more specific they are, the more quickly you can react when things go wrong.

- *Don't check in broken code*: Checking in often is great, but don't overdo it. Don't check in code until it works, and never check in broken code. If you need to switch context, use the "suspend" feature in TFS to put things aside for a while.

- *Fix broken builds immediately*: If you happen to break something, it's your responsibility to fix it.

- *Write unit tests*: The system needs to know that works and what doesn't. Unit tests and other inspection tools should be used to make sure the code does more than just compile.

- *All tests and inspections must pass*: With inspections in place, you must pay attention to the results. Use feedback mechanisms to make people aware when something is broken.

- *Run private builds*: If you can do a test build before check-in, in you can avoid committing things that don't work.

- *Avoid getting broken code*: If the build is broken, don't get the latest code. Why work on code that's broken? Instead, use the version control system and specifically get the latest version that worked.

Components of Continuous Integration

Now you know what CI is all about. Or do you? What does a CI process consist of Compiling code to a set of deployable files? Running unit tests? Build automation with integrated running of unit tests is a great start, but the CI process can be more than that. Figure 6-3 shows a process we consider a complete CI solution. This should be what you strive to achieve.

Continuous Integration

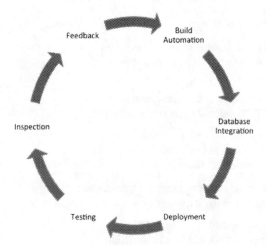

Figure 6-3. *The Continuous Integration cycle*

Let's drill down into each of these components in more detail.

Build Automation

Build automation is the core step in the CI process. The automated build system is typically used to drive the CI process, not just to do compilation and execute unit tests. Anyone with permissions to do so should be able to trigger an automated build at any time, and it should be possible to set up a schedule for builds (such as nightly builds). The build process should also publish the build results in a central location so people can get builds easily as well as look at the build status.

Automating the build process isn't always a trivial task, but the benefits it gives are many:

- Saves time

- Reduces errors

- Provides predictable results

- Helps you learn about problems early

- Reduce dependency on individuals

Any new project should implement an automated build skeleton, because having the foundation in place from the start makes it much easier to do the right thing.

When implementing automated builds, you also need to think about what kind of build you need in which scenario. It's common for development teams to have more than one build setup for a branch, which may include the following:

- *CI builds*: Lightweight builds that provide feedback quickly; often incremental, with limited testing

- *Private builds*: Builds that test changes to be committed before they're checked in

- *Nightly builds*: Complete builds with more exhaustive testing

- *Release builds*: Complete builds with release notes

Database Integration

Another area that often takes a lot of time in the deployment process is database integration. Traditionally, updating databases as part of a change is a manual process in which either the developer writes database change scripts or a DBA performs a comparison between two known database versions and then runs the upgrade manually.

However, there are ways to integrate this process into the CI process. For instance, if you can run a tool that performs a comparison and generates a change script, you should be able to teach the build process to do that automatically. If you're afraid your environment won't work if the process fails, you can protect against that by automatically running a backup before the upgrade; then, should something fail, you can have the build process restore the database to its previous state.

Deployment

In order to use the build result for manual or automated testing, you need to deploy the build onto an environment. The deployment process can be as simple as copying over a set of files to the target environment, or it may require local installations on multiple machines. But there are tools and techniques to solve any of these challenges; you typically simply have to spend time learning about the steps involved in getting a release installed.

Testing

When the software has been deployed, you can run tests on it. The core compile phase of the build process typically runs the unit tests; but you should run regression tests on a realistic environment with proper test data available. Ideally you want a process in which you can run automated build-verification tests after every deployment in order to verify that the software works well enough for your testers to spend time testing it. After that you can add more automated regression tests if you find value for them; the process of running them as part of the CI process will be the same.

Inspection

Integrating all these steps is great, but how do you know if something goes wrong? Compiler errors and failing tests can easily be trapped and visualized. But what about code quality? Can you, for instance, fail a build if the code coverage for unit tests is below an agreed-on level? Or if the code becomes more difficult to maintain over time, can you be notified? The CI process is like the heartbeat of the project, and you can take advantage of this when it come to inspection. Some inspections should lead to immediate action—for example, compiler errors should fail the build. Others can be reported to a central location so you can look at the trends later: for instance, code metrics and overall build status.

Feedback

The last step in the process is a good way to notify the team about what works and what needs to be looked at. A good feedback system provides visibility about issues immediately so you can fix them before they grow into big problems. Be as creative as possible about making the build result visible to the team: maybe display it on a build monitor or send out email alerts.

ALM 2.0+ and Visibility

ALM 2.0+ stresses visibility because visibility helps stakeholders understand the progress and quality of your development projects. Many organizations tightly couple software innovation to a competitive advantage. Releasing new products, finding new distribution channels, and improving customer engagement all require the use of software. With real-time access to project status, you can make informed decisions about the direction you're heading. With rapid changes to business priorities, you may also need rapid changes in your development direction. Without visibility, this isn't possible. To make this happen, you need ALM and ALM tools that can help you manage these changes.

ALM 2.0+ stresses shared measures as well. Lack of visibility into what each development group is doing is often the root cause of mistrust between groups in organizations. ALM 2.0+ provides transparency by enabling teams to build dashboards that clearly define operational, process, and development metrics. It also allows developers to correlate this information using meaningful reports. Transparency across the application's life cycle (including feature usage, operational tickets, and common usage problems) improves release decisions and influences what new functionality teams implement.

You also need support for historical data, according to ALM 2.0+. Effective planning requires a view that includes not only today's information but also past information. ALM 2.0+ tools provide the ability to store historic views of estimates, actual effort, task burndown, and productivity, allowing teams to make better, more-informed decisions about future work and to use real information to continually improve processes.

ALM 2.0+ also lets you collect data from many different practitioners' tools. These tools may be build systems, systems to track work items, test-management systems, and so on. Many of these tools provide valuable application insights. For example, code-complexity tools assess the architectural complexity associated with code. Aggregating that information provides a view of a system's overall complexity. ALM 2.0+ tools marshal information from today's wide array of practitioner tools.

Automating Visibility

You can of course achieve visibility manually, but doing so is tedious and error prone. It can work for small teams or small projects; but once the team or project grows in size, you can easily lose track of traceability if you try to manage it manually. Luckily, there are many tools on the market that can help you.

Using a good ALM tool helps you gather project information in a central repository. Microsoft Team Foundation Server uses a central database called the TFS warehouse. All relevant project data is kept in this database and can be retrieved either through standard reports and graphs or via custom-made reports using, for example, Microsoft Excel. It can also help you retrieve information by providing reports and letting you construct your own reports. So, when considering your ALM toolset, keep visibility automation in mind. It's well worth the investment to have a toolset to assist you.

Traceability

Traceability in software development usually means linking requirements (coming from the stakeholders) to code, builds, test cases, and so on. With traceability, you can support software-development activities like change-impact analysis, compliance verification or traceback of code, regression-test selection, and requirements validation. A common way to do this is by using a requirements traceability matrix (RTM). But keeping such a matrix updated and current at all times is hard and requires considerable manual work. Instead, you should look at an ALM tool to help you do this in an automated way.

A software traceability matrix document (Figure 6-4) can take many different forms, but one of the most common is a table-like document that serves as a graphical representation of all the cross-referenced links between project deliverables and artifacts, and the code.

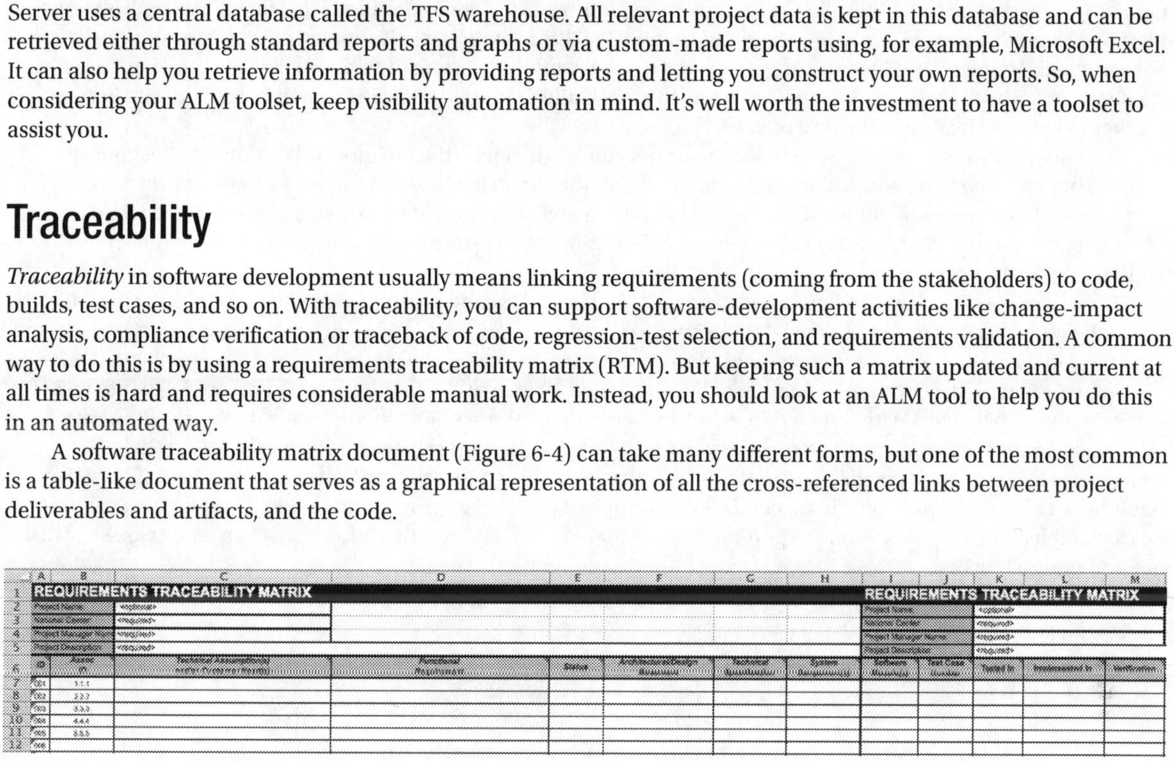

Figure 6-4. An RTM example in Microsoft Excel

This cross-referenced table is usually constructed using a spreadsheet program like Excel. You list the relevant software documents and then the code unit as columns, and each software requirement as a row. You see more about this later in this chapter.

From this, you can figure out that traceability in software development really is requirements traceability. Let's take a deeper look at this concept.

Software Traceability

Traceability as a general term is the "ability to chronologically interrelate the uniquely identifiable entities in a way that matters" (http://en.wikipedia.org/wiki/Requirements_traceability). Traceability has been around longer than software engineering; its meaning originated from other practices like farming, where food is tracked from a specific farm to a final destination shop; and the medical field, where it's essential to track drugs from the factory to the patient.

An important aspect of traceability is the ability to trace where requirements came from, how you've satisfied them, how you've tested them, which build they're part of, and what will happen if they're changed. These are all important aspects of software development.

Keep in mind that traceability goes both ways. You need to be able to track *from* the requirements as well as *to* the requirements. This is a key concept in traceability.

When developing software, there are usually many sources of requirements. The business side, end users, marketing department, and other stakeholders all have requirements for the product. Most often, the requirements differ between these people, and having good traceability enables you to track the person or group in your business that wanted the implemented feature in the first place. For example, if a user study shows that a feature isn't used, you can determine why the feature was required to begin with. Going back to the original stakeholder, you can discuss whether to keep the feature in the next release.

Traceability also provides great benefits during development. It may not be important to know *who* requested a feature but rather to know *where* the requirement is implemented. That way you can easily track where in code a requirement has been implemented so you quickly can find what portion of code needs to be changed when an original requirement is changed. This also helps you determine what test cases need to be changed to reflect the requirements change.

If you have good traceability, you can also trace what part of the code broke a build and more quickly find the part of the code that you need to correct. If traceability is automated in your ALM solution, you can use the tool so you don't have to do manual work to find the right place in the code.

Figure 6-5 shows a very simple example of how traceability can work. A requirement is broken down into tasks, which the developers work with. When they check in a task, they (or the ALM system) associate the check-in with a changeset in the version control system. There are also test cases (and test plans) associated with a task. Each changeset is included in a specific build and turned into executable code when it's built. You get traceability from a requirement all the way to a specific executable, including test cases, changesets, and builds. This way, you can trace the executable(s) in which a specific requirement was implemented and use this information, for example, when implementing a bug fix.

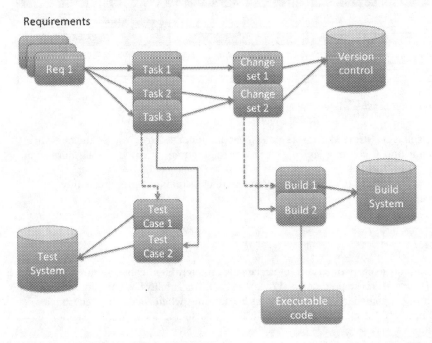

Figure 6-5. Simple example of traceability

Most people involved in software development recognize these situations. You need to be better at traceability so you can deliver better-quality products that are at the same time easier to maintain.

Requirements traceability focuses on the relationship between the requirements and the development artifacts (models, test cases, builds, executable code, check-ins, documentation, and so on) to help you do the following:

- Improve the overall quality of what you're developing

- Improve your understanding of the product during development

- Improve your ability to handle changes

Software development is, like so many other aspects of life, highly dependent on relationships. Details such as user requirements, functional requirements, test cases, and other items that define the scope of what you're building are related in some fashion, either directly or indirectly. Figure 6-6 shows an example of a common (traditional) process flow.

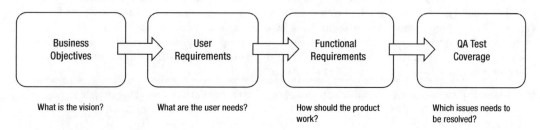

Figure 6-6. *Common software-development process flow*

Using trace relationships, you can connect these items together to map out the interdependencies among them. These relationships are the foundation for doing traceability effectively. But not only the process steps are important. People are also involved, and it's important to connect them as well. Why is that? Well, behind all requirements are real people—customers, stakeholders, end users, and project team members—who are important to the realization of the requirements. When one requirement changes, a chain reaction goes down the line. To better ensure the success of your project, you need to keep track of this effect. That's one of key reasons to use traceability.

ALM 2.0+ Supports Software Traceability

Let's now take a look at how ALM 2.0+ supports traceability. Traditional ALM was very focused on artifact traceability, which linked requirements, test cases, code, builds, and so on. ALM 2.0+ extends traceability to an even wider view of the application, including operations.

Many customers we have met over the years have problems with traceability. They find it very hard to know where and how an update or a bug fix will have an effect. Lacking traceability, a bug fix to one part of a system may cause a new bug somewhere else. With no (or poor) traceability in place, the only real way to find any surprises is to test, test, and test some more. As one customer said, "I have no way of knowing how a transaction really is routed through our applications today. Implementing a small bug fix cost too much money and effort because we need to test so much when implementing it. The effect of this has been that we have stopped doing updates in our old system unless the update is really critical for the organization."

Obviously this isn't a good way to manage an organization's IT systems. In ALM 2.0+, the goal is to provide the organization with a good understanding of undocumented assets and runtime dependencies. To manage this complex traceability, ALM 2.0 supports the following:

- *Integration with multiple repositories*: The ALM 2.0+ solution should be a hub for information that is stored in different repositories. The information may be stored in the operations system, the development system, and so on but is accessible from the ALM 2.0+ solution. This way, you can bring development and operations closer together, which is an important aspect of the DevOps movement in recent years.

- *Collecting data from many practitioners' tools*: This can be a challenge because many different tools are available for development organizations. Think about all the different developer coding tools: Visual Studio, Eclipse, and database tools, just to mention a few. All these tools collect information that gives you insight into your application(s). If you aggregate this information, you can get a view of how complex your systems really are. However, this is hard to do manually; a good ALM solution must be able to help you. It's also difficult to do this with an ALM tool unless standards are set for how you communicate between applications. In many cases, different tool vendors use different, sometimes proprietary, ways of exposing their information. Often you must perform custom development to can integrate these different information sources if your tool isn't ready to help you.

- *Traceability that evolves as the team works*: If you've created an RTM at the start of the project, you need to keep it updated as the project moves on. The initial traceability is constantly replaced as the team works. This means the ALM 2.0+ toolset must allow you to view the information in the software assets in different ways over time. One way to accomplish this is to tag assets in a way similar to social media sites like Twitter and Facebook. This gives you great flexibility when searching for information. An example of how this can be implemented is shown in Figure 6-7. Microsoft TFS allows tagging of work items; and because all work items can be linked to each other as well as test cases, builds, code, and so on, you can easily search and find important information.

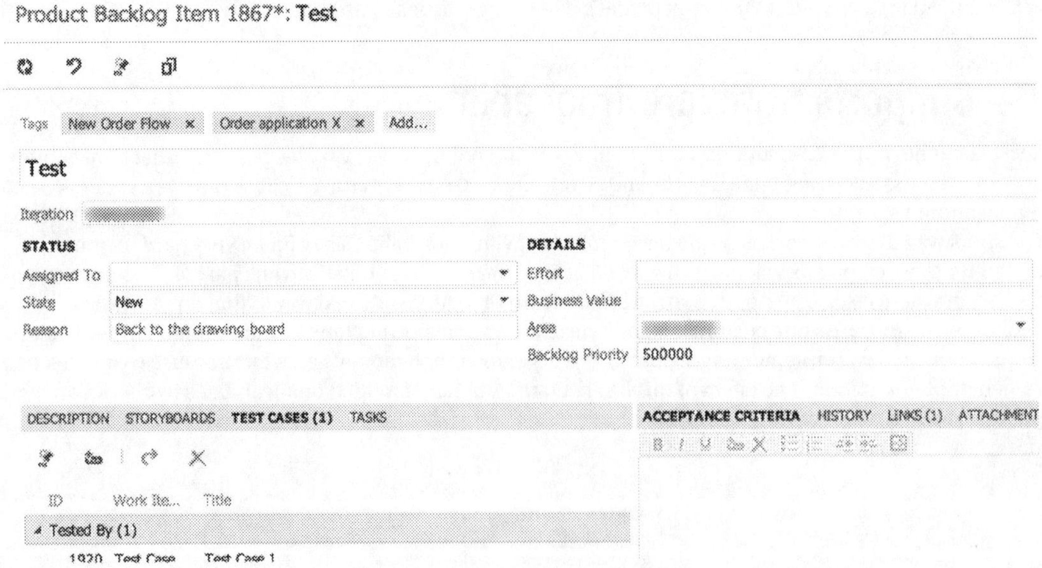

Figure 6-7. Tagging a work item in Microsoft Team Foundation Server

Why Traceability is Important

Without a good toolset helping you, traceability can be very time consuming and costly. But even if you don't have a good tool helping out, *not* having traceability costs even more in the end. Consider two scenarios we often experience:

- While running an agile project, you may have a situation where the product owner wants to change an already-implemented business requirement in a coming sprint. (Managing these changes in a good way is the whole point of agile frameworks, so you constantly have this situation in these projects.) If you don't have good traceability, how can you know exactly which part of the code you need to change? How can you know which test cases you need to change? How can you know what other parts of the application will be affected by the change? Traceability helps you answer these questions and also helps you cut the costs and effort involved in implementing the change.

- Close to the launch of an application, you may find a serious bug in a popular feature. Do you ship with the bug or take care of it at once? With poor traceability, it's harder to know who is working on that feature. Who else needs to be notified and weigh in on the decision? What else does it affect? As you can understand, significant costs are involved in solving this situation if you don't have control of your traces.

When you consider whether to invest in traceability, you also need to consider the costs involved down the line if you don't have it. Most often, the costs are higher when you don't make the initial investment. Consider the customer we mentioned earlier that stopped doing bug fixes in its older systems. You don't want to end up in that situation: not only is the cost of testing high, but you may also lose business opportunities because you can't easily adapt to changes in the business processes needed to keep your competitive edge.

One other benefit of traceability is having a comprehensive audit trail of changes, so you can analyze who, what, when, and why a change occurred. At the same time, you can easily roll back to an earlier version if needed, because it's all stored in the unified system of record.

Even if you choose to manage traceability manually, it offers several valuable benefits to organizations:[1]

- *Minimize risk*: Assess risks and the overall impact of a change before it's made.

- *Control scope changes*: Manage change throughout the process, and avoid scope creep.

- *Reduce development costs*: Avoid gold plating and costly engineering rework.

- *Increase productivity*: Keep the team in sync, and reduce administrative overhead.

- *Provide complete test coverage*: Ensure that all requirements are properly tested before a release.

- *Achieve greater visibility*: Gain end-to-end visibility into the process for the entire team and stakeholders.

Agile Frameworks and Traceability

Many agile teams use tools that help them collect build and integration information in their CI flow. This improves visibility into the build process and also traceability because the tools often allow the team to see which requirements, work items, and tests each build included.

---

[1]John Simpson, "Connect the Dots: Five Tips on Requirements Traceability," *Business Analyst Times*, Nov. 16, 2009, www.batimes.com/articles/connect-the-dots-five-tips-on-requirements-traceability.html.

Agile teams often use test-driven development and increase the importance of test artifacts. Business analysts and quality assurance practices are converging, which is something agile methods encourage. Agile's emphasis on the definition of "done" and frequent inspection increases the desire to link work items with test plans and cases. The result is that agile teams create simpler, more traceable, requirements and see higher integration with test assets.

Automating Traceability

You can track traceability manually using Excel or any other spreadsheet application, but doing so is time consuming and requires hard work. There are also many other tools on the market that will work.

By using a good ALM tool that can help you automate the traceability process, you can boost productivity significantly. Automating traceability also help you minimize the risk of human errors. Figure 6-5 showed a simple example of how traceability can work. Just imagine this setup without the use of a supporting tool that automates the process—it would be a nightmare. An ALM toolset can integrate all the information in one place so you don't have to do custom integrations to collect data.

When you're considering an ALM toolset, keep traceability automation. It's well worth the investment.

Summary

This chapter stressed the importance of visibility and traceability. *Visibility* is the ability to measure progress or status against goals. It's important for understanding the status of projects. Having greater visibility enhances your ability to change heading and keep your competitive edge.

Many agile processes help with visibility because they stress the need to focus on build and release practices. Agile teams plan frequently, which gives them more information about project health. Agile teams also view and use this information on a daily basis and change course if necessary. Visibility in an agile environment allows teams to use information in their stand-ups, sprint reviews, demos, and retrospectives.

One of the most popular agile practices is continuous integration, which enhances visibility as well as traceability. Agile frameworks like Scrum and XP supports traceability in many ways. You've also seen that ALM 2.0+ supports traceability and has it as one of its pillars. Good traceability helps you minimize risk, control scope changes, reduce development costs, increase productivity, provide complete test coverage, and achieve greater visibility. For an even better traceability process that's less prone to human error, we recommend investing in an ALM toolset that helps you automate traceability.

Our next chapter will discuss some aspects of how automation of processes can help us increase our software development process.

CHAPTER 7

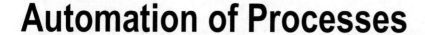

Automation of Processes

Improving quality is very important for any software development organization in order to be successful. Quality can, of course, include many aspects. We often discuss two types of quality:

- *Functional quality*: How well the software complies with the design, which is itself based on a set of functional requirements or specifications.

- *Structural quality*: How well the software complies with the nonfunctional requirements that support the functional requirements. This includes maintainability, robustness, and so on.

Productivity, and being able to boost productivity along the way, are also important in software engineering. At the same time, it's important to make sure quality doesn't suffer as productivity increases.

Another key area in software development is keeping your projects on track. How can you get transparency into your projects so that you can more easily see their current status? If you don't know the status, you can't make the necessary decisions to keep your projects heading in the right direction.

There are two ways you can go when managing processes in an ALM solution. You can handle them manually, or you can automate them. Unfortunately, manual processes are error prone and rely on human interaction. It's easy to forget something when you're right in the middle of software development; if one or more steps of the process are forgotten, it affects your ability to know the project's current status. One example is a simple thing like forgetting to link a check-in to a specific user story. Suddenly, traceability suffers. This could be disastrous during later development as well as during operations when the software is deployed.

By automating your ALM solution and the processes within it, you can avoid many of the pitfalls of handling them manually. You can, for instance, make sure it isn't possible to check in code without linking to the user story the developer was working on. You can also use automated reporting that collects the current project status in a report and publishes it on a web page so everybody interested can see it.

Helping the development team not spend time on unnecessary manual steps by automating them frees time for the team. They can spend that time on development instead, thus increasing productivity.

The project-management process is a large part of any ALM process, as you saw in Chapter 2. Therefore it's important to consider which process best suits your organization and how you can automate it. Personally, we prefer agile methods, because they have done so much to improve project success rates over the last decade. We think there is no better way to develop and maintain software right now than by using an agile approach. Fortunately, there are tools that can help you automate these processes.

An automated process help retrieve the feedback you need in order to constantly improve and adapt so you can ship high0quality software to your customers. This goes hand in hand with the agile concepts of continuous feedback and adjustments.

The DevOps movement has received a lot of attention recently. Many organizations are striving to improve in this area because DevOps drives integration between two parts of the organization: operations and development. These two parts have traditionally been separated from each other, which is odd considering that they actually are closely connected. The development teams produce software that operations manages. They can't be separated, because the quality of the software affects the operations team's ability to maintain it.

Several tools on the market can help you automate your processes. And we don't only mean project-management process; we're talking about build, test, deploy, and other processes, as well. Keep in mind that the tools should help you, not be a hindrance to you—so choose them wisely.

This chapter discusses process automation in more detail and explains why it's important. It also discusses how you can benefit from process automation by looking at the build and release cycle specifically.

What Is Process Automation?

Let's take a closer look at what process automation means, particularly from an ALM 2.0+ perspective. There are many processes in the application life cycle that you can automate. Let's start with the project-management process.

Project-Management Process

ALM 2.0+ stresses that your toolset should allow you to follow many different project-management processes. In many organizations, more than one process is available for this task. Agile is the most recent and popular process, of course, but there are others, like the Rational Unified Process (RUP), Waterfall, Microsoft Solutions Framework (MSF) for agile, Capability Maturity Model Integration (CMMI), and so on.

These processes cover the development process, but beyond this are portfolio-management processes, operations processes, release-management processes, and demand processes, just to mention a few. This means teams need ALM to manage many differing, overlapping, and complex process models.

A good ALM toolset should help you automate processes as well as enable you to implement workflows across several different tools. This means the toolset should let you, for instance, integrate your development process (for developing software) with a good test process and on to operations through your release process.

In order to increase your visibility into project status, it's important that the toolset also capture metadata for the tasks performed in the development process. Usually you want to track a task (coming from a specific requirement) by following its effort (how hard it is to perform), its size (how big it is), the work remaining until it's finished, its risk, perhaps its business value, and, of course, its result (for instance, the final executable code or test results). Having the ALM tool gather this data and provide reports that let you view the data is invaluable to any project.

Changes to processes and workflows occur constantly, so it's also essential for your toolset to be flexible so you can adapt to these changes in the system.

Because most organizations use different tools for development, you need your ALM solution to be able to work with different practitioner tools. This means in an ideal world, you shouldn't have to rely on a single vendor's tools for development but instead should be able to choose the tools you want and integrate your workflows and processes across all tools using the ALM system. We think we have a way to go to accomplish this. Mylyn (`www.eclipse.org/mylyn`), for instance, provides an interesting approach by taking responsibility for the process "glue" as a third party. This allows vendors to build processes within their tools and use Mylyn to integrate those processes.

Test Process

You should strive for seamless integration with automated build and test tools. This has a positive effect on increasing quality. Tasks—many of which are often invisible to software practitioners—commonly require a large amount of time and effort to execute.

Let's look at unit testing, for example. Unit testing is a software testing method in which the developer (or tester) writes tests that cover a specific part (unit) of the source code. This could be a function or a procedure or even a module. Often a unit can be viewed as the smallest testable part of an application. Unit tests are typically written and run by software developers to ensure that code meets its design and behaves as intended. You can also create user interface (UI) tests that can be automated so you aren't limited to tests of pure code.

Ideally, each test is independent from other tests so you don't have too many dependencies to other modules, functions, or procedures. This makes it easier to see if an error belongs to the specific code that is being tested.

When changes are made to the code, you can run the unit tests again and see if any bugs have been created. This can be tedious work if you have to run the unit tests manually, so they're often automated for better efficiency. Once automated tests have been developed, they can be run quickly and repeatedly. Many times, this can be a cost-effective method for regression testing of software products that have a long maintenance life. Even minor patches over the lifetime of an application can cause existing features to break that were working earlier.

In many ALM tools, you can connect the build process to your unit tests. This means you can run automated unit tests before building the software and find any failed tests before you deploy a new build. This way, you can fix the problem and perform a build that runs all tests without failure. Some ALM tools also let you run automated tests before a check-in, in which case you can find any errors even earlier in the process.

ALM 2.0+ provides the means to execute this type of automation and also facilitates rapid-release approaches that exploit new technologies such as virtualization and cloud resources. Let's look next at the build and release cycle.

Build and Release Process

An integrated ALM 2.0+ solution reduces manual processes, handoffs, and documentation—and, consequently, many of the mistakes that creep into the deployment process. It also allows for more-frequent delivery. By using the same technology and process to move code in development that is used to make the final move to production, an ALM 2.0+ solution can make this process more robust.

Packaging software for release can be a complex, process-oriented, document-centric activity for app dev professionals. Developers often deliver to operations out-of-date information that bears little relationship to the release's software components.

The next section shows you the value of automating processes using continuous integration (CI) as an example. Let's look at how you can improve on the CI concept from Chapter 6 and further enhance it using continuous delivery (CD).

Continuous Delivery: A Process-Automation Example

Chapter 6 covered CI and demonstration its benefits. Continuous integration does the following:

- Improves project visibility
- Reduces risks
- Reduces manual routines
- Creates shippable software
- Improves confidence in the product
- Identifies deficiencies early
- Reduces time

Figure 7-1 shows a complete CI solution and should be what you strive to achieve.

Continuous Integration

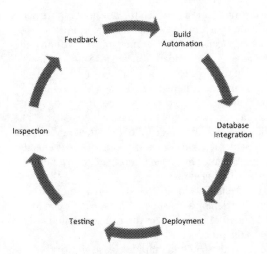

Figure 7-1. *Continuous integration circle*

CI is a good example of how you can automate and integrate processes in your toolset. The problem with CI isn't that it's not a good solution: it's that it can be a solution to a nonexistent problem. Deployment as part of the CI flow isn't just about automating the build, test, and release process. You need to think about delivery, to add value to the deployment process.

CI gives you a framework for efficiently producing software in a controlled fashion. But to get the most out of it, you need to look at how it fits into the overall process of delivering software. In an agile project, you want to deliver working software in every iteration. Unfortunately, this is easier said than done; it often turns out that even if you implement CI and get the build process to produce a new installation package in a few minutes, it takes several days to test a new piece of software and release it into production. How can you make this work better?

The "Null" Release Cycle

What is the "Null Release" really? If we changed one line of code in our application (or system), how long would it take us to deploy it into production using our regular release process? That time is the "null" release cycle. Often we strive to shorten this lead-time by improving how we deliver code changes.

The following example assumes that you have a project where the code is already in production and is being maintained by an operations team. Let's start by asking the following simple question:

How long does it take to release one changed line of code into production?

The answer is most likely much longer then you'd like. What stops you from improving? First, you must know more about how you release your product. Even in organizations that follow good engineering practices, the release process is often neglected. A common reason why this happens is simply that releasing software requires collaboration across different disciplines. To improve the situation, you need to sit down as a team and document the steps required to go from making a code change to releasing the software into production. Figure 7-2 shows a typical delivery process: in practice, work happens sequentially, just as shown.

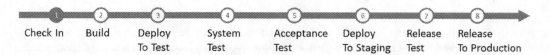

Figure 7-2. *A typical delivery process*

Having come this far, you know a lot more about the delivery process, which means you can start optimizing it:

1. Look at the steps in the process that take the longest, and see what can be done to improve that time.

2. Look at the steps in the process that most often go wrong, and understand what is causing the problem.

3. Look at the sequence of the steps, and think about whether they need to be run in sequence.

Having looked at the process and asked the questions, you can now design a better process, such as that shown in Figure 7-3.

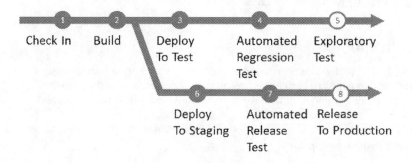

Figure 7-3. *An optimized delivery process*

In this model, we have changed the process so that most steps are automated, by implementing automated tests as well as automated build and deployment. Releasing to production automatically isn't for the fainthearted, so this is done manually, but using the same automated scripts as the automated deployment to the test and staging environments. We do believe, however, that it's possible to automate even the release to production, especially if you've had this process working since the first iteration of the project. By doing so, you build up confidence in the process; having seen it work throughout the development cycle should allow you to trust the process even at this critical stage.

In Figure 7-3, we've also parallelized the acceptance test and preparation of the production environment. By doing these in parallel, you can push the release to production as soon as the acceptance tests are green, instead of doing the traditional stage to production first after the acceptance tests have passed.

If you're interested in real-life examples of what we've discussed here, many are available on the Internet. One example is Flickr, which has released some information about how it does this. Watch this Tech Talk video for a start: http://vimeo.com/24542044.

Release Management

CD is a great practice to produce updates in a controlled and effective manner. But without an intentional release-management discipline, you can lose much of its value. What you need to add to the picture is the way release planning ties into the deployment process and ensures that you know what features you want to deploy where and when.

A Scrum project is a good situation when it comes to release management, because the first thing you do is create a product backlog; then you continuously groom the backlog as part of the project cycle. In other words, the backlog can be your release plan. If you don't work with Scrum, you need to use other means to create a release plan so you know which features you're going to deliver when.

With a release plan in place, you can design your delivery process to support the project's different phases. If you need concurrent development, you can implement a branch strategy to support it, but this is outside the scope of this book. With multiple branches, you can add CI builds to keep the code clean, your environments up to date, and so on. Based on the release plan and the CI process, you can even automate the release notes for every release you do.

Things to Consider Before Automating Processes

Let's now look at some things you should think about before you automate too much. Automation is good, but there are aspects you should consider before going too far with an ALM solution.

Benefiting from an ALM Solution

Implementing an ALM tool for automation can be costly. You need to obtain software licenses, train staff on the new toolset, and so on. Make sure the work required to put the tool in place doesn't outweigh the benefits they provide. Don't let the tool force you or your teams to do things they wouldn't have to do without the tools. Think about this pillar of agile:

> ***Individuals and interactions*** *over processes and tools*

> —Agile Manifesto (http://agilemanifesto.org)

Tools can be a tremendous help, but don't let them be a hindrance to your teams. Tools should work for you, not the other way around.

Using Different Tool Vendors

If you use an ALM solution from a single vendor, you can probably go a long way with automating your processes. But keep in mind that other parts of the organization involved in software development (such as business analysts [BAs] who are gathering requirements) use other tools. Their tools may not support process integration with your ALM suite. In the BA example, the development team may ship the wrong things because process integration and automation failed or were nonexistent.

Know the Weaknesses of Your ALM Tool

ALM solutions on the market today can help you automate many processes. However, they can't do everything for you. When deciding on a toolset, take a moment to evaluate what processes the tool can help you automate and what the benefits will be. Once you've made the decision, get to know the toolset so you can avoid potential pitfalls.

ALM and DevOps Is Still a Struggle

According to Jean Louis Vignaud, ALM Segment Lead at IBM Rational, there are gaps in extending ALM to DevOps: "You can speed the development process, but if deployment is not fully integrated to the development process it will lead to defects and errors. So expanding the development cycle to deployment is where the industry still has some gaps."[1]

"There's definitely a move within DevOps for automating the ability to deploy into production, but automation starts sooner than that," said Carolyn Pampino, Program Director, Strategic Offerings for IT Software Delivery, IBM Rational. "The analogy for DevOps is you can focus on making one train move faster, which is typically what automation is about, or you can focus on how to coordinate all of those trains. From a DevOps perspective, you need that direction."

Summary

This chapter has focused on process automation. It offers considerable benefits, because manual steps are often error prone and tedious.

One key issue with automation is how to use your toolset to automate processes that span different parts of the development process. You saw an example of using continuous deployment to integrate and automate building, testing, and deployment into one automated flow.

To our knowledge, no vendor has an overall automation solution that covers all aspects of ALM. This means in real life you may find yourself in a situation where you have different tools from different vendors and can't integrate them with your ALM solution. So, you must evaluate which solution or vendor will help you the most.

The next chapter shows how ALM can help you with work planning.

---

[1]Colleen Frye, "Automation in ALM: Avoiding a Negative ROI," TechTarget, March 2012, http://searchsoftwarequality.techtarget.com/feature/Automation-in-ALM-Avoiding-a-negative-ROI.

CHAPTER 8

Work Planning

These days, delivery frequency is increasingly rapid to adjust to an ever-changing reality. This means teams need to manage their work more frequently, as well. Disconnected work-planning activities that aren't integrated into the workflow, reporting, and traceability of an organization's development processes have become impractical. As more and more teams start using agile processes, their need for integrated planning activities increases as well. A good ALM 2.0+ solution can help. Let's look at some of the ways you can use ALM to better plan your work.

Task Management

Tasks play an important role in ALM 2.0+ because they allow for traceability and work planning. This also leads to higher visibility. Many tools can help here, such as Mylyn, IBM Rational Team Concert, Microsoft Team Foundation Server, and so on. Why are tasks so important, and how can they help you?

Sometimes it seems that we hundreds of sticky notes on our monitors and desks, each containing at least one task we're supposed to do. Often it isn't possible to track them with a tool. It could be that some tasks are connected with one project, and other tasks are part of another project. We could try putting them all in a spreadsheet and saving that to a computer. But soon we may find that the spreadsheet is located on a laptop, a customer's computer, a desktop, another customer's computer, and so on, and we have no idea which one is the current version. This can be a real problem if we have no clue which version to trust.

The same thing happens with projects. Project managers have to-do lists for projects, and they all have their own way of keeping the lists updated. Let's say a PM uses Excel to keep track of tasks: the status of each task, whom it's assigned to, and so on. How can the PM keep the team updated with the latest to-do list? If the PM chooses to e-mail it, chances are some teach members won't save the new version to disk or will miss it in the endless stream of e-mails coming into their mailbox. Soon various versions are floating around, and things are a mess.

One way to solve this is to use a project web site running on Microsoft Office SharePoint Server or a similar tool. This can help, although you may still get in trouble if people forget to save changes or check in documents after updating them.

Another problem may occur if, for example, an Excel spreadsheet is updated by a tester who discovers a bug and changes the status of one entry in the task list to indicate that a developer should look at the task again and solve the bug. How can you alert the developer that the bug exists? You want this action to take place automatically, right? That's difficult if you use only an Excel spreadsheet. The same thing occurs the other way around: when a developer fixes a bug, you want the tester to be alerted that the problem has been resolved, so the tester can check whether the bug can be closed.

What about requirements traceability? If the only place you keep track of the connection between requirements and code is in a document, how do you know the document is updated? Can you trust the information?

Even if you purchase a tool to help you keep track of tasks, it's still a separate tool for each category of team members. There are tools for bug tracking, requirements management, test management, and so on—the list is long. Chances are, someone will forget to update the tool because it takes too long to open, because it's too difficult to work in, or due to one of many other excuses. This could cost the project money and time.

Tasks or Work Items

Most ALM solutions provide a task-tracking system. Figure 8-1 shows a backlog in HP Agile Manager, which is one of the products in HP's suite of ALM tools. It helps control tasks.

Figure 8-1. *HP Agile Manager*

The core of this system is represented by the tasks themselves, which are sometimes known as *work items*. Different vendors may use different names, but let's use *work items* here. A work item can be pretty much whatever you want it to be: a bug, a requirement of some sort, a general to-do item, and so on. Each work item represents an object that is stored in the ALM tool data warehouse. It often has a unique ID that helps you keep track of the places it's referenced (see Figure 8-2).

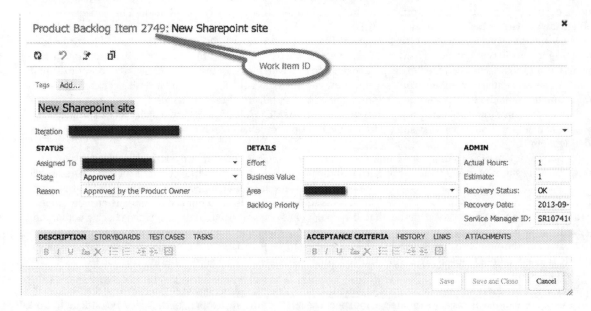

Figure 8-2. *Each work item has a unique ID in Microsoft Team Foundation Server*

In Figure 8-2, you can see how Microsoft implements work item IDs. Figure 8-3 shows what this looks like in Pivotal Tracker.

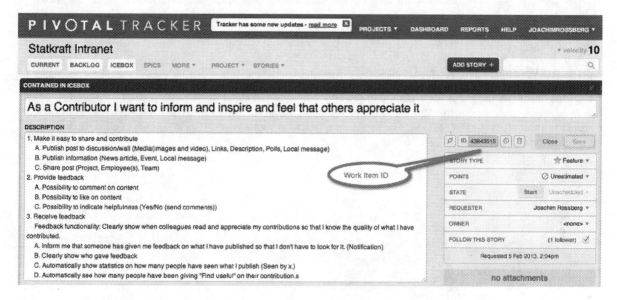

Figure 8-3. *Work item ID in Pivotal Tracker*

The ID lets you follow one work item (let's say a requirement) from its creation to its implementation as a piece of executable software (component), assuming the ALM tool does what you want it to do. Work item IDs should be unique across all work item types in all projects in your ALM system. A good ALM solution lets the work item type determine the work item fields that are available for tracking information, defaults defined for each field, and rules and constraints positioned on these fields and other objects that specify the work item workflow. Every change made to a work item field is stored in the work item log, which maintains a historical record of changes.

Work items provide a great way for you to simplify task management in a project while at the same time enabling traceability. No more confusion about which version of the task list is the current one. No more manual labor, gathering status reports on work progress that are used only at steering-group meetings. Now you have a solution that lets you collaborate more easily with your team and enables all members and stakeholders to view status reports whenever they want. Having this data available historically as well allows you to plan coming work more efficiently.

A flexible ALM toolset should let you tailor work items as you want them. You should be able to modify work items in the project so they contain new information that you need. If you need to report some information that the project or stakeholders require, you should be able to tailor the system accordingly.

All work items can have different information attached to them. This may include information about the team member to whom the work item is assigned and the status of the work at the moment (for example, a bug could be open, closed, under investigation, resolved, and so on).

You should also be able to attach documents to work items and link one work item to others. Some tools let you create a hierarchy of work items. Let's say you implement a requirement as a work item, and this requirement contains many smaller tasks. You can put the requirement at the top and nest the other requirements below it so you know which work items belong to which requirement.

When a bug is discovered, you can quickly follow the original requirement based on its work item ID and see where in the code you may have to make fixes. You can also see the associated work items so that you can evaluate whether other parts of the code need to be changed as a result of this bug fix.

Because many ALM tools save information about work items in a data store, you can see the history of each work item: who created it, who resolved it, who closed it, and so on. The information in the databases can be displayed in reports, which you can tailor depending on your needs. One report may show the status of all bugs, for instance. Stakeholders can see how many open bugs exist, how many have been resolved, and much, much more. It's completely up to you how you choose to use work items.

Planning Work Using Work Items

With all the information in your work items, you can create reports that allow you to make plans for the project. If you run your project using Scrum, the ALM tool can aggregate the remaining work logged on each work item and create a burndown chart (see Figure 8-4) to help you see how much work remains in the sprint as well as when (a date) all the planned work will be ready.

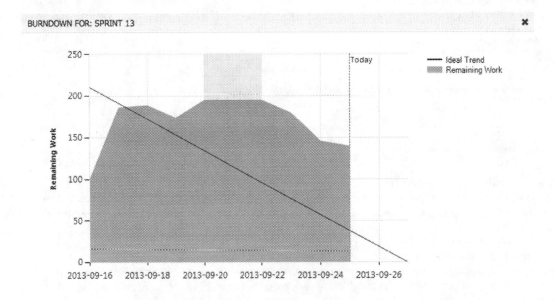

Figure 8-4. *A burndown chart created by Microsoft Team Foundation Server. In this example, you can see that the team has a lot of work left in the sprint and may not be able to reach the sprint goal*

Many ALM tools also help you visualize how many sprints are left to work through the backlog. Often, teams estimate the size of user stories by estimating in story points. Once you know how many story points the team can finish in a sprint (the average of how many story points the team has historically finished in each sprint), you can get a pretty realistic view of what stories will end up in the coming sprints and how many sprints are required to finish all the work (see Figure 8-5). For a product owner, this information is essential when planning resources and coming releases. The PO can easily see how adding or removing items or reordering the backlog will affect the coming sprints. Based on this, the PO can visualize the effects of changes to the backlog.

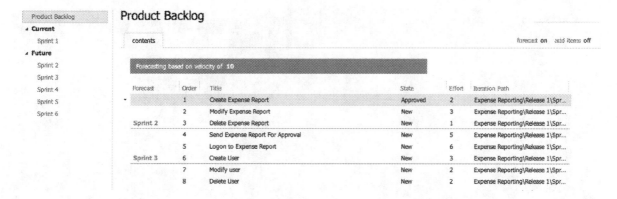

Figure 8-5. *In this figure, the backlog reflects which items will end up in which sprint*

With the information you now have about work items and how you can use them, let's see how this can help you further.

Reporting that Resolves Estimates and Actuals

As you can understand from the previous section, teams can capture both estimated and actual effort. This is particularly important for agile teams, because they use this information to refine estimates and predict project length. It's important that your ALM 2.0+ tools supply real-time information, allowing you to change the project's course when necessary and to compare estimates to your actual figures when any new work comes in.

ALM 2.0+ Enables Good Planning Functions

ALM 2.0+ requires that the toolset include good planning functions. ALM 2.0+ tools should provide functionality to define tasks and allocate them to resources by including data that helps your project. Work items are the foundation for all information in your projects. They can help you get a better understanding of the status of your projects, programs, and, of course, releases. The planning functions that ALM 2.0+ tools support don't replace the strategic planning functions provided by enterprise architecture and portfolio management tools, but they give you a mechanism to execute and provide feedback on those strategic plans.

Support for Historical Data

In order to more effectively plan your projects, you need access not only to actual statistics but also to historical data. You should be able to store historical data about estimates, actual effort (if you care about that), burndown speed, and so on. This allows you and your teams to make better, well-informed decisions about upcoming work. In the end, this will help you improve your processes.

Figure 8-6 shows a cumulative flow chart. This is a tool used in queuing theory: it's an area graph that depicts the quantity of work in a given state, showing arrivals, time in queue, quantity in queue, and departure (http://en.wikipedia.org/wiki/Cumulative_flow_diagram). Cumulative flow diagrams are often seen in the literature for agile software development and lean product development.

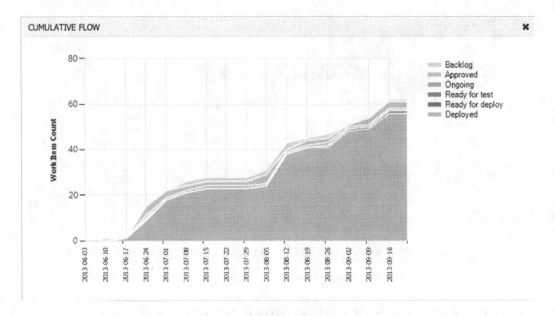

Figure 8-6. *A flowchart showing the cumulative flow of a project*

A cumulative flow chart can help you with two things. First, it helps you find typical information about the status of work: how much work is finished, ongoing, and in backlog; the pace of progress, and so on. Second, once you understand the chart, it helps you spot all sorts of issues your team may be facing. This is where cumulative flow diagrams show their real value.[1] If your ALM tool didn't enable you to collect this information and also automatically create the report for you, you'd have to do a lot of manual labor to reach this level of understanding about a project.

Summary

In this chapter, you've seen how ALM can support work-planning activities in the projects you run. One of the key things is to be able to collect information about the tasks (or work items) in your projects. Using this information, you can better plan the future of those projects using both historical and current data.

The next chapter shows how ALM can enhance collaboration among team members, stakeholders, and any other parties with an interest or stake in your project(s).

---

[1]For more information about this type of chart, see Pawel Brodzinski, "Cumulative Flow Diagram," July 15, 2013, http://brodzinski.com/2013/07/cumulative-flow-diagram.html.

CHAPTER 9

■ ■ ■

Collaboration

More and more, we see teams from separate geographic locations working together. Large organizations today have development teams in different countries and sometimes on different continents. If you work for such an organization, you may find yourself in a situation where day-to-day interpersonal communication isn't possible. You need to find other ways to collaborate.

Not just communication can be a challenge in such an organization. Sharing and working on the same code base from different locations is also difficult. How can you set up a continuous delivery process? This situation obviously demands that your ALM solution supports a distributed environment without the tool itself becoming too complex and requiring too much extra infrastructure or overhead.

Your ALM solution must enable your team members to work, interact, share information, and collaborate effectively to the extent that they feel almost as if they're collocated. This is a real challenge for ALM vendors.

Handling geographically spread teams isn't the only challenge, either. In order to develop high-quality software, you need ALM tools that help different parts of the organization work together: for instance, supporting the business side as well as the development side, supporting operations as well as development, and so on. Without good collaboration across organizational units (or, perhaps better, silos) your projects can suffer greatly.

This chapter discusses some aspects of collaboration in which you can use ALM tools to enhance your project quality and deliver higher business value to your users and organization. It doesn't cover all aspects of collaboration but instead shows some of the quickest ways to enhance quality and business value by enabling collaboration.

Let's start with a hot topic these days: DevOps, where development teams partner with operations staff to ensure that software deploys and runs with a minimum of problems. This approach aims to increase collaboration between these two parts of an organization and is definitely in line with an ALM strategy.

After that, you look at how you can increase collaboration by including the business side to a greater extent in your development work. The chapter ends by looking at the importance of sharing information.

DevOps

Many companies struggle because a distinct separation exists between the development and operations areas. Most often this is visible when development comes to the end of a project and is ready to deploy software into the production environment. Suddenly the project team realizes it should have included the operations team earlier—the operations team isn't ready to accepting the software because the team members lack input and information regarding the new system. It isn't uncommon for operations to have problems with delivery because the architecture of the new system requires new infrastructure. This leads to delays and confusion and probably a bit of frustration on both sides as they try to work it out—especially because the situation could have been avoided if the operations side had been included earlier and given feedback on early design reviews. Let's take a look at what DevOps is and how it can help you.

DevOps Overview

DevOps tries to overcome problems like those just described by creating a partnership between the development and operations areas. This is of course where the name *DevOps* comes from. Briefly, the dev team(s) supports many operational requirements by supplying deployment scripts, load and performance testing, diagnostics, and so on right from the start of a project. In return, the operations team(s) provides support from day one of the project. The operations team should also be given the chance to provide feedback on the architecture and design. Frankly, this sounds so obvious to us that we wonder why organizations haven't been doing this for years.

DevOps includes the release cycle, so quality assurance (QA) aspects are important in this area as well. Figure 9-1 shows how DevOps includes all these areas.

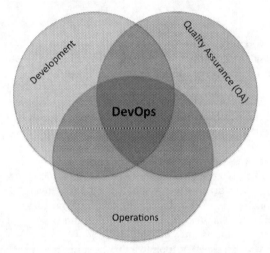

Figure 9-1. *DevOps covers development, operations, and QA*

DevOps is a way to become agile during software deployment. By having close collaboration during a project, using short, regularly scheduled meetings, you aim to combine development and operations to collaboratively and continuously deliver business value. This approach also shortens the feedback loop, giving you time to react quickly and adjust when necessary. Many organizations with a clear DevOps approach also collocate developers and operations staff to further enhance its benefits. DevOps can be seen as a set of processes and methods for thinking about communication and collaboration between departments, not just as a deployment process.

There is no special method or process for DevOps. Many organizations use known agile methods like Kanban and Scrum. The key concepts are continuous development, continuous integration, and continuous deployment. These are all concepts you recognize from the agile world. By working with short increments instead of long project cycles (as with the Waterfall process), removing many manual processes, and replacing them with automated processes, you can achieve a more optimized development flow, allowing you to deliver high-quality business value regularly. The time from idea to production is most often key to enabling the organization to make money, and DevOps teams strive to optimize the flow to achieve this.

DevOps teams also strive to make sure the development and testing environments are as similar as possible to the production environment so debugging and testing can be done effectively. So, not only does DevOps strive for better collaboration between development and operations, but you also get enhanced collaboration with QA. In combination with short release cycles, this lowers the risk of each deploy (see Figure 9-2).

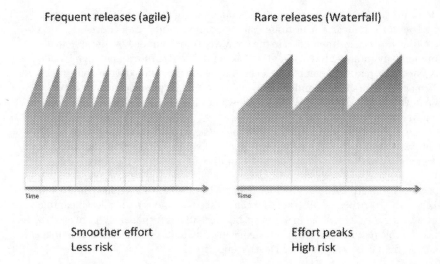

Frequent releases (agile)

Time

Smoother effort
Less risk

Rare releases (Waterfall)

Time

Effort peaks
High risk

Figure 9-2. *Agile frameworks shorten the release cycle compared to traditional processes like Waterfall, allowing quicker feedback loops*

But suppose your operations team uses Information Technology Infrastructure Library (ITIL). Can you really use DevOps? This is a question we often get when talking to customers. ITIL and DevOps are not contradictory. You can safely use them both. Combining them allows you to be more effective by automating change and release management and connecting the constant-improvement process from ITIL with agile development methods. Using DevOps, standardized changes are more frequent, hence decreasing the need for heavy and time-consuming change organizations and meetings.

How Well Has Your Organization Adopted DevOps?

How far has your organization come on the DevOps path? Three simple questions can help clarify your status. They don't provide a complete assessment, but they do give you a hint about where you stand:

- Do developers have access to troubleshooting information in real time?

- Does the production environment use tests and other tools originating from the development team to validate that the production environment is running as it should?

- Do the developers view the network/infrastructure team as a partner?

If your answer is "no" to these questions, you have a way to go yet. If you have one or two "yes" answers, you have begun the walk.

How Can You Start Adopting DevOps?

There are a few things you should consider when adopting DevOps ideas. As you can see from the discussion so far, DevOps is more about culture and processes than it is about organization. Culture is hard to change in any organization, but as with the successful adoption of an agile mindset, you need to work on your soft skills to fully succeed at a DevOps implementation. It can be tough to break down the barriers between two organizational areas that traditionally have been separated; but if you make it, you'll be rewarded with higher-quality software and more satisfied users.

The tools you use can help enforce processes so they become an integrated part of your daily job. You can use tools to implement best practices such as, for instance, sharing troubleshooting information across development and operations. You can do this by adding more instrumentation in the software so you can see how the system is performing not only in your development environment but in QA as well as in production. *Instrumentation* is code that catches errors, report timeouts, checks system parameters, and so on during the execution of your code. It's written to logs and can be shown using development tools and monitoring tools. This helps you catch any code problems quickly, which in turn allows you to fix defects faster. Thus the feedback loop is faster, and you can be more agile and responsive to business requirements and changes.

Using continuous delivery, as discussed in Chapter 8, lets your ALM tools tie developers and operations staff together more tightly. There are many ways your tools can help you, so check the abilities of the tools you already have; if they can't support you well enough, you should perhaps consider another toolset. But what you have can probably take you a long way.

Even though a specific DevOps professional role may not be specified, having one isn't a bad idea. The Toyota Production System (http://en.wikipedia.org/wiki/Toyota_Production_System) includes a Chief Engineer role. This person has no formal authority over the teams involved in a project, but instead has responsibilities related to the project's success. To accomplish this, the role requires technical knowledge in order to direct and convince managers regarding project needs. Such a role may help you succeed with a DevOps adoption.

▓ **Note** The *Toyota Production System* (TPS) is an integrated socio-technical system developed by Toyota that comprises the company's management philosophy and practices. TPS organizes manufacturing and logistics for the automobile manufacturer, including interactions with suppliers and customers. The system was a major precursor of the more generic *lean manufacturing*. Taiichi Ohno, Shigeo Shingo, and Eiji Toyoda developed the system between 1948 and 1975.

Originally called *just-in-time production*, TPS builds on the approach created by the founder of Toyota, Sakichi Toyoda, his son Kiichiro Toyoda, and engineer Taiichi Ohno. The principles underlying it are embodied in The Toyota Way (http://en.wikipedia.org/wiki/Toyota_Production_System).

Engaging the Business Side

If the gap between development and operations traditionally has been wide, the gap between the business side and development has been even wider, at least in many organizations. For some reason it's been a hard struggle to get these two parts of an organization to communicate the requirements and expectations for a new system. The result has been devastating to project success over time, and many stakeholders and end users have ended up feeling that they haven't received the system they wanted.)

A recent example was a new system for the Swedish police force, called Pust Siebel. This project began in 2009 and was meant to be a new issue-reporting system for police officers working in the field. They were supposed to be able to easily report crimes directly from their vehicles using laptops. The first part of the project was built using open source, Java, and agile methods. It was very successful and was considered a really good system by most police officers.

But in 2011, after having spent between $13 million and $14 million, management decided to close the project and restart it, standardizing on the Oracle platform Siebel. This decision was immediately strongly criticized internally in the police organization. But nevertheless, management decided to go ahead, and development began using more traditional development methods rather than the previous successful agile approach.

Throughout development of the Siebel version of Pust, management chose to ignore feedback from users that the system was a pain to use. Things that previously took minutes to perform now could take hours. By the end of 2013, the criticism was so strong that management decided to stop the project after having spent another large sum of taxpayer money.

Most of the stories we've heard from people with insight speak of a project where management chose not to listen to users and stakeholders in the organization. By not integrating the project development team with the business side, the outcome was a system that was user unfriendly, slow, and basically useless, as opposed to the successful agile version.

Better Collaboration between Development and Business

It is of course easy to complain about a situation, but how can you improve it? In our opinion, one of the most significant means of improvement comes with using agile methods. Why? Because one cornerstone of the agile principles is collaboration with, and inclusion of, the business side.

Scrum has the role of the product owner (PO), for instance. This role is a direct link to the business side. A PO is responsible for the outcome of a project, for its ROI, and for it delivering business value to the organization (see Chapter 4 for more on this). In order to perform this role, the PO must anchor all project decisions with stakeholders throughout the organization.

In the best of all worlds, the PO is a person from the business side with a mandate to make decisions regarding the project they are responsible for. If the PO takes this role seriously, you'll have good collaboration between the business side and the development side of the organization.

Requirements Gathering

Because the PO is responsible for the outcome of a project, it's also the PO who needs to have control over the requirements from various parts of the organization. This can be done in many ways, and I will describe one way I've seen this work.

In a company I was working with (as a PO proxy), we scheduled fixed stakeholder meetings with participants from different departments that were involved in the system in one way or another. Before these meetings, any stakeholder could use a template to submit a request for a feature or a feature change. This way we knew that each request stood up to a certain level of quality, and we then discussed them at the meeting. When we met, we let the submitter present the request, and then we discussed whether we should go for it. We were able to get feedback from the entire organization, and we could also prioritize the different requests so the PO had a good backlog in shape for the sprint-planning meeting.

To describe requests, we sometimes used storyboarding with great success. Let's take a closer look at this, because it's a great way to enhance collaboration.

Storyboarding

Storyboards have long been used as a tool in visual storytelling media—films and television especially, although graphic novels and comics are perhaps an even closer analogy. Storyboarding is used in software development to help identify software specifications. During the specification phase, screens that the software will display are drawn, either on paper or using other specialized software, to illustrate the important steps of the user experience. The storyboard is then modified by the engineers and the client while they decide on their specific needs.

There are several tools you can use to create storyboards. Microsoft offers a PowerPoint Storyboarding add-in, and Balsamiq offers tools as well.

In the book *Storytelling for User Experience* (Rosenfeld Media, 2010), Whitney Quesenbery and Kevin Brooks offer these benefits of using stories in software design:

- They help you gather and share information about users, tasks, and goals.

- They put a human face on analytic data.

- They can spark new design concepts and encourage collaboration and innovation.

- They're a way to share ideas and create a sense of shared history and purpose.

- They help you understand the world by giving you insight into people who aren't just like you.

- They can persuade others of the value of your contribution.

Storyboarding is useful during software engineering because it helps users understand exactly how the software will work, much better than an abstract description could. In addition, it's cheaper to make changes to a storyboard than to an implemented piece of software.

Stories are an effective and inexpensive way to capture, relate, and explore experiences in the design process, regardless of whether you're talking about user experiences or other requirements. Storyboards visualize what the stakeholder wants and provides an opportunity to talk about requirements in a different way than if you only used written requirements. You can, for example, walk through the flow of a system using storyboards and gather input from stakeholders.

Continuous Feedback

Agile frameworks can be beneficial in other ways as well when it comes to collaboration. Agile teams work in a highly collaborative, self-organized environment. An individual's ability to adapt to new practices and processes plays an important role in their success on the team. Timely feedback about a person's actions from fellow team members can help the person to course-correct to meet project objectives, while also helping keep the team environment and culture positive and supportive.

Such feedback, when provided much later during annual or half-yearly performance reviews, is seldom useful in helping people succeed on projects. In self-organized teams, the practice of continuous feedback can drastically shorten the feedback loop for individuals and put them on the path of continuous improvement. It also fosters a healthy environment of openness and honest feedback among team members, which is critical for an agile team to learn and adapt quickly to perform at their best potential.

But it isn't only within the team that feedback is essential. It's also essential for communication between the stakeholders responsible for requirements and the development team. One of the strengths of agile is that after each iteration there is a sprint review (in Scrum terminology), giving stakeholders the opportunity to see the direction the project is going and provide feedback. This gives the team a way to adjust to the feedback and steer in another direction if necessary.

If your ALM tools can help in this process, it's great. One example is the Microsoft Feedback Client (Figure 9-3), which is a tool that allows a developer to send a feedback request to a stakeholder (or any other person) requesting feedback about a feature. The Feedback Client allows the stakeholder to launch the application and capture the interaction using video, voice, written comments, screenshots, and so on. The client can then send the feedback back to the developer, and Team Foundation Server stores everything, providing traceability for the feedback.

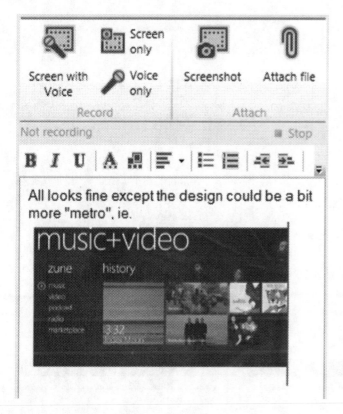

Figure 9-3. *Microsoft Feedback Client*

Chapter 10 looks at some metrics in ALM that can, if supported by your ALM tool, give you good continuous feedback on the status of your projects.

Sharing Information

With teams often spread geographically, it's important to manage what information should be shared and how the project should share it so that everyone can see it.

Maintaining a Shared Backlog

Most teams use some kind of backlog for the work at hand, regardless of whether they use agile methods. Chapter 4 took a closer look at the agile use of a backlog.

Many tools can help you maintain a backlog. JIRA Agile from Atlassian is one (see Figure 9-4), and Microsoft Team Foundation Server is another (see Figure 9-5).

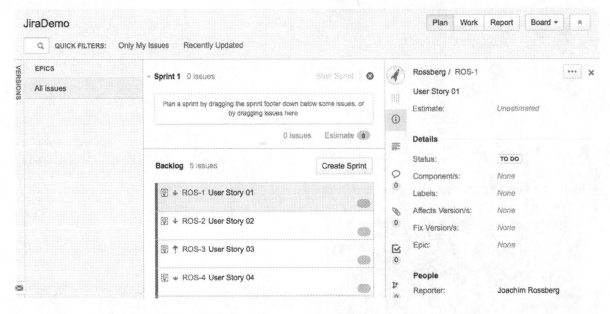

Figure 9-4. *Maintaining a backlog using JIRA Agile*

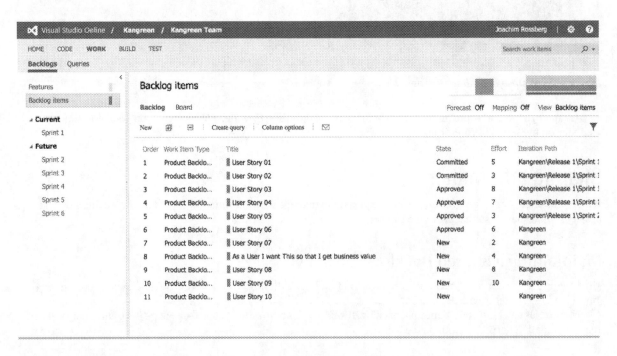

Figure 9-5. *Maintaining a backlog using the online version of Microsoft Team Foundation Server, called Visual Studio Online*

There are other tools you can use as well, such as Pivotal Tracker or the simpler Trello, but they work in similar ways. You use the backlog tools to enter all requirements (often in the form of user stories) into the list as described earlier. The PO can then prioritize (order) the list as desired. The development team or anyone else interested in the backlog (stakeholders, other teams, and so on) can access the backlog, as long as they have an account or client-access license, and view the current status of the project. This not only enables collaboration across a geographically dispersed team but also enhances visibility into the project.

We've had great success on projects with participants from different countries working against the same backlog shared across the Internet. At standups or sprint planning meetings, we've been able to use the digital backlog efficiently. Some may argue that nothing beats being collocated, but real-life situations in many organizations don't allow that; and in those cases, a digital backlog is a great way to be able to collaborate effectively.

Sharing Documents and Information

In addition to having a shared backlog, you can use Microsoft SharePoint to share document libraries containing important documentation that isn't part of the user stories. To share documents, you can use Google Docs or a similar service.

Most companies have some kind of solution for sharing documents and information. Because many of the projects we've been part of have involved participants from various organizations, it has been essential to enable access for all users. Make sure your ALM solution includes an option for this.

Summary

This chapter has focused on collaboration and how you can enable better collaboration using ALM tools. We have mainly looked at how to better collaborate between the business side and the development side and between development and operations. Many of the practices we've seen stress not only tools to accomplish collaboration but also importance of personal interaction.

With geographically dispersed teams, it's important to be able to collaborate effectively. Using agile practices, digital backlogs, and well-integrated development tools and practices, you can be very successful in enabling collaboration within your teams and organization. This will make it possible for you to increase the quality and business value of your releases.

Let's now continue looking at some important ALM metrics and what they mean for your success.

CHAPTER 10

■ ■ ■

Metrics in ALM

A *key performance indicator* (KPI) is a performance measurement used in most organizations to evaluate the organization's success or the success of a particular activity within the organization. Often, KPIs are used to measure the effects of a change project—for instance, implementing a good ALM process—or to evaluate the progress of a development project.

You can use the score from an ALM online assessment as a KPI and compare the assessment scores before and after the implementation of an ALM process improvement. This way, you get an indication of whether you have improved due to implementing a new process.

During projects, you should also be able to use the reports from your ALM toolset to determine whether you're constantly improving your work. Continuous improvement, in our opinion, is something to strive for. When it comes to project management, you can, for instance, look at the team's velocity (how fast the team is able to work) and see if it's growing or decreasing. By using reports and metrics from your ALM tools, you can choose the KPIs you want and learn how to evaluate them.

This chapter looks at metrics for five topics that cover most aspects of software development:

- Project management

- Architecture, analysis, and design

- Developer practices

- Software testing

- Release management

Keep in mind that many of the sample reports we show here are taken from Microsoft Team Foundation Server. The reason is that it's a platform we work with frequently, and hence it's easy to use as a base to show reports with good data. Most of these reports are of course available in other ALM tools as well. They may be named differently, but the same data and information can often be retrieved.

Project-Management Metrics

To get good metrics about the status of your projects, it's important to measure your progress. You can do this in several ways. If you're using agile as a methodology, many of these metrics and reports should be familiar. To others, they may be new.

Agile Metrics

Let's look at some important reports that are commonly used in agile practices:

- Backlog overview

- Sprint burndown

- Velocity report

- Release burndown

- Remaining work

- Unplanned work

The *backlog overview report* lists all user stories, filtered by tags and iteration and in order of importance. Basically this is a list of user stories filtered by the criteria you need. Many people use Excel (or another spreadsheet application) to create this report, but many ALM tools have built-in support for producing it. Figure 10-1 shows an example from IBM's Agile Manager.

Figure 10-1. *The backlog overview report in IBM Agile Manager*

We've mentioned the *sprint burndown* before (see Figure 10-2). This report shows how much work there is left to do in a sprint. Using it, you can predict when the team will be finished with the work assigned to this sprint, either in the sprint or after the sprint is finished. Based on this information, the team and the product owner (PO) can take actions to make sure they deliver what they have committed to.

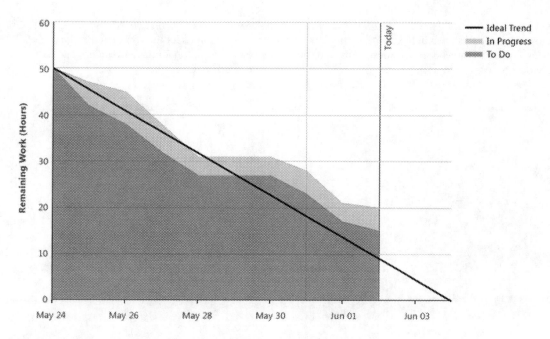

Figure 10-2. *Sprint burndown report*

The *release burndown chart* (Figure 10-3) shows the same thing as the sprint burndown, but for the work included in a release.

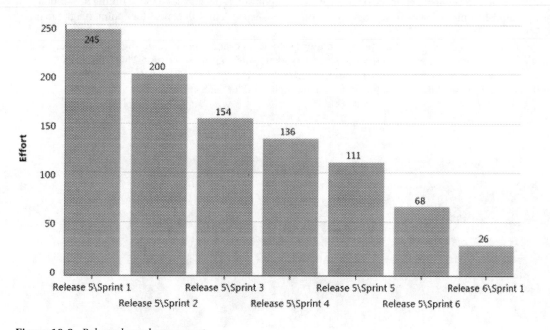

Figure 10-3. *Release burndown report*

A *burndown and burn rate chart* (Figure 10-4) is another way to show a project's burndown. No surprises here: this is the same information shown in Figure 10-1. The burn rate provides summaries for the completed and required rate of work for a specified time period. In some tools, you can also see the information for team members. You can sometimes choose to see the report based on hours worked or number of work items.

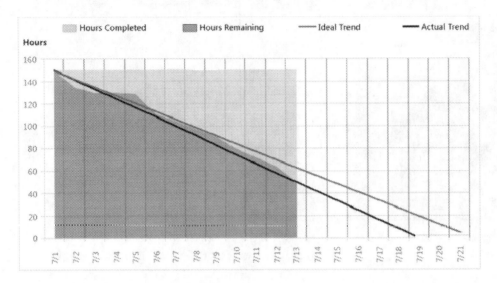

***Figure 10-4.** Burndown and burn rate report*

Velocity (how much work a team can take on in a sprint) is important, especially for a PO planning how much work can be accomplished in coming sprints. Velocity is usually a measure of the effect per story point that the team can accomplish.

Before any work is started, the PO calculates a theoretical velocity in order to begin planning. As time goes by, it's updated with the team's real velocity based on how much work they deliver in each sprint. This helps the PO estimate how much work the team can take on in coming sprints. The *velocity chart* (Figure 10-5) can help you easily retrieve this figure. Here you see how much effort the team has delivered for each sprint.

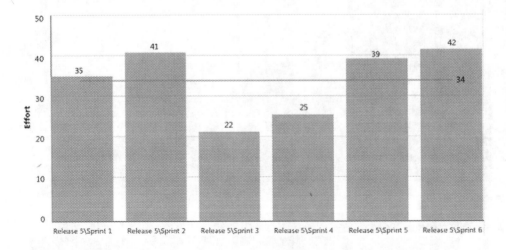

***Figure 10-5.** Velocity report*

Remaining work (Figure 10-6) is another great report. You can use it to track the team's progress and identify any problems in the flow of work. In some tools you can view this report in either an Hours of Work view or a Number of Work Items view.

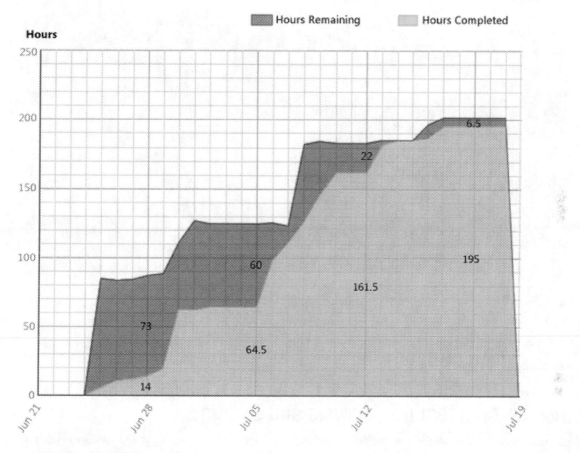

Figure 10-6. *Remaining work report*

The *unplanned work report* (Figure 10-7) is useful when the team plans an iteration by identifying all work items that they intend to resolve or close during the course of the iteration. Work items assigned to the iteration by the plan completion date of the report are considered planned work. All work items that are added to the iteration after that date are identified as unplanned work.

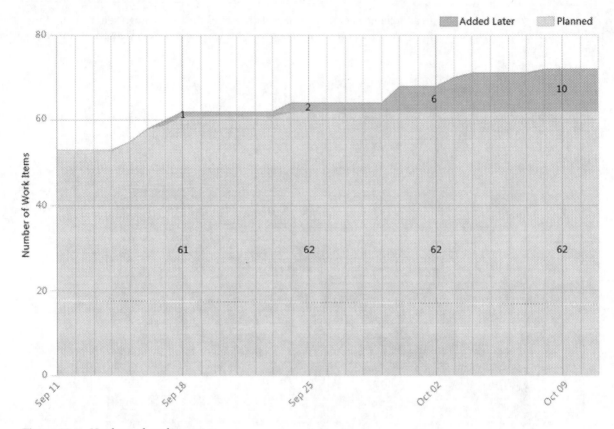

Figure 10-7. *Unplanned work report*

Metrics for Architecture, Analysis and Design

ALM tools don't include many metrics you can use for KPI assessment for architecture, but you can use some taken from the development area. Using the code metrics, you can get information about how your architecture and design are working, including the following:

- *Lines of code*: This is an approximate number based on Intermediate Language (IL) code. A high count may indicate that a type or method is doing too much work and should be split up. This may also be a warning that code will be hard to maintain.

- *Class coupling*: Measures the coupling to unique classes through parameters, local variables, return types, method calls, generic or template instantiations, base classes, interface implementations, fields defined on external types, and attribute decoration. Strive for low coupling; high coupling indicates a design that is difficult to reuse and maintain because of its many interdependencies on other types.

- *Depth of inheritance*: Indicates the number of class definitions that extend to the root of the class hierarchy. The deeper the hierarchy, the more difficult it may be to understand where particular methods and fields are defined and/or redefined.

- *Cyclomatic complexity*: Determined by calculating the number of different code paths in the flow of the program. It indicates the code's complexity. A high complexity makes maintainability suffer, and it can also be hard to get good code coverage.

- *Maintainability index*: An index value between 0 and 100 that represents the relative ease of maintaining the code. The higher the better: a rating above 60 is good. Below that, maintainability suffers.

Some ALM tools can generate dependency graphs. These graphs are used to visualize code and its relationships. Running analyzers on these graphs can give you useful information as well:

- *Circular references* are nodes that have circular dependencies on one another.

- *Hubs* are nodes that are in the top 25% of highly connected nodes.

- *Unreferenced nodes* have no references from any other nodes.

Using these analyzers, you can see if you have loops or circular dependencies so that you can simplify them or break the cycles. You also can see if you have too many dependencies, which could be a sign that they're performing too many functions. To make the code easier to maintain, test, change, and perhaps reuse, you need to look into whether you should refactor these code areas to make them more defined. You may also be able to find code that performs similar functionality and merge with it. If the code has no dependencies, you should reconsider keeping it.

Metrics for Developer Practices

Metrics for developer practices are KPIs that can help you understand if you're successfully working to improve your code. These are useful from both the architectural and design viewpoints as well as from a developer viewpoint. Using them will help you improve how you design your application or system.

Several important metrics are available automatically in many tools and can help you get a good understanding of the quality of your development work:

- Code coverage

- Code metrics

- Compiler warnings

- Code-analysis warnings

Code Coverage

Code coverage shows you how much of the code has been covered by automated unit tests. You get the value as a percentage of the entire code base. The difficulty often is deciding what percentage is enough. Should you always strive for 100%, or is 80% enough? This is something the team has to discuss with the PO in Scrum or a similar decision-maker in other processes. This value is input for the Definition of Done (DoD).

Code Metrics

You can look at several different code metrics:

- *Lines of code* is an approximate number based on IL code. A high count may indicate that a type or method is doing too much work and should be split up. This may also be a warning that code will be difficult to maintain.

- *Class coupling* measures coupling to unique classes through parameters, local variables, return types, method calls, generic or template instantiations, base classes, interface implementations, fields defined on external types, and attribute decoration. You should strive for low coupling because high coupling indicates a design that is difficult to reuse and maintain due to of its many interdependencies on other types.

- *Depth of inheritance* indicates the number of class definitions that extend to the root of the class hierarchy. The deeper the hierarchy, the more difficult it may be to understand where particular methods and fields are defined and/or redefined.

- *Cyclomatic complexity* is determined by calculating the number of different code paths in the flow of the program; it shows the complexity of the code. High complexity makes maintainability suffer and can also make it difficult to achieve good code coverage.

- The *maintainability index* is an index value between 0 and 100 that represents the relative ease of maintaining the code. The higher the better. A rating above 60 is good. Below that, maintainability suffers.

Compiler Warnings

Errors and warnings should be avoided in a project. Allowing more than zero errors or warnings tends to result in the team accepting lower quality in the codebase, which over time causes the code to lose maintainability (commonly known as the *broken windows theory*).[1]

Track this metric to make sure the number of errors is zero. This should ideally be enforced by automatic build policies.

Code-Analysis Warnings

Code analysis in development tools performs static analysis on code, which helps developers identify potential design, globalization, interoperability, performance, security, and many other categories of potential problems. Much of this is so far only available for .NET development; if you're using Java, things may be different.

Code-analysis tools provide warnings that indicate rule violations in managed code libraries. The warnings are organized into rule areas such as design, localization, performance, and security. Each warning signifies a violation of a code-analysis rule.

Code analysis can be used to enforce company policies on the code developers write. Many ALM tools offer good support for code analysis, usually including a set of rules. Often you can even extend them by writing your own rule set or suppress the rules you don't want. Definitely discuss this with your development team and the PO, because the warnings have an impact on the effort required before the DoD is fulfilled.

---

[1]See http://en.wikipedia.org/wiki/Broken_windows_theory.

Metrics for Software Testing

Software testing is an important area. Testing should be a constant part of any development effort and not only a phase at the end of the project. There are good metrics you can use during your projects to make sure you have high-quality testing in place.

Follow are a number of metrics you can use as KPIs for software testing:

- *Number of bugs per state*: How many bugs are active, resolved, or closed? Is the number of active bugs increasing and the number of resolved and closed bugs constant? If so, you need to look into how you perform your testing.

- *Number of bugs sent back from testers for more information (a.k.a reactivated bugs)*: A large number may indicate that communication between developers and testers must improve.

- *Code coverage*: This shows how much of the code has been covered by automated unit tests. You get the value as a percentage of the entire codebase.

- *Tests run results*: How are your tests performing? Do you have many failed tests? If so, what can you do to improve this?

- *Percent requirements covered by test cases*: Do you write test cases for all your requirements? If not, what is the reason?

- *Percent requirements covered by testing*: Do you actually run the tests for which you have test cases? If this figure is low and the figure for *percent requirements covered by test cases* is high, you may have an issue you need to deal with.

Example Reports

The metrics you get in your reports concerning testing can be very helpful in your projects. The reports described here are found in many tools:

- Bug status
- Reactivations
- Bug trend

Bug Status Report

The *bug status report* gives you information about the cumulative bug count based on bug state, priority, who it's assigned to, and, of course, bug severity. It shows you the number of bugs and the number of resolved bugs (see Figure 10-8 and Figure 10-9).

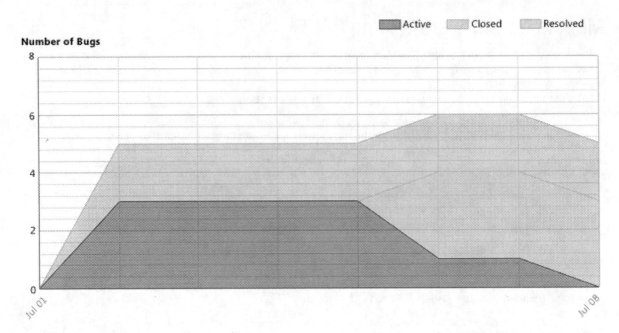

Figure 10-8. *Bug status report*

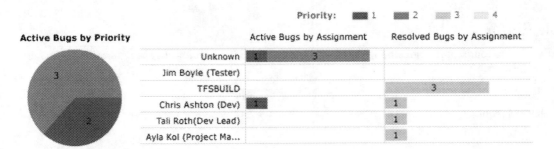

Figure 10-9. *Bug status report*

Figure 10-8 shows the number of bugs over time. You can see how the numbers of active, closed, and resolved bugs have changed. In this case, the number of active bugs is decreasing and the number of closed and resolved bugs is increasing, leading to a point where the number of active bugs is 0.

Figure 10-9 shows a report that displays how many bugs are assigned to an individual user. You can also see the priority of each bug as well as how many bugs have been resolved by the users.

Reactivations Report

The *reactivations report* (see Figure 10-10) is used to see how many bugs have been resolved or closed too early. If a bug needs to be opened again, it's called a *reactivation*. A high number indicates that the developers need to improve their bug-fixing process and not close or resolve the bugs unless they really are ready to be closed. It can also be an indication that you have bad communication between testers and developers. For instance, incomplete test reports and poorly written test cases can cause this.

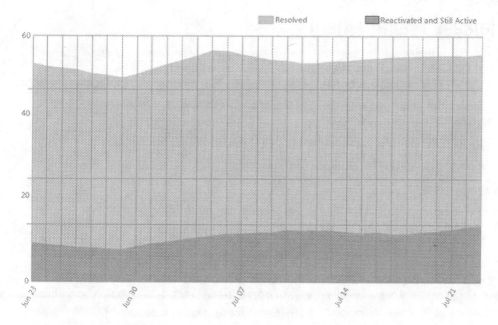

Figure 10-10. *Reactivations report*

Bug Trend Report

Next is the *bug trend report* (see Figure 10-11). This report helps you track the rate at which your team is finding, resolving, and closing bugs.

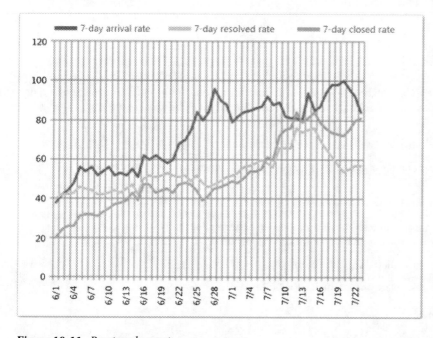

Figure 10-11. *Bug trend report*

Metrics for Release Management

A quick look at the Information Technology Infrastructure Library (ITIL) (www.itilnews.com/ITIL_v3_Suggested_ Release_and_Deployment_KPIs.html) will give you some other KPIs you can use. If you want to use them, you may need to create your own reports to automate the retrieval of this information. ITIL mentions these KPIs, among others:

- Number of software defects in production (the number of bugs or software defects of applications [versions] that are in production

- Percentage of successful software upgrades (excludes full installations)

- Number of untested releases (not tested and signed off)

- Number of urgent releases

- Average costs of release, where costs most likely are based on man-hours spent

---

▓ **Note**   The ITIL, is a set of practices for IT service management (ITSM) that focuses on aligning IT services with the needs of business. ITIL describes procedures, tasks, and checklists that aren't organization specific, used by organizations to establish a minimum level of competency. It allows an organization to establish a baseline from which it can plan, implement, and measure. It's used to demonstrate compliance and to measure improvement.

Sample Reports

Following the progress of your builds is essential in order to keep track of quality. These reports differ from ALM platform to platform, but let's look at some examples from Microsoft Team Foundation Server 2012. Use them as inspirations for what you can look for in your platform:

- Build quality indicators

- Build success over time

- Build summary report

The *build quality indicators report* (see Figure 10-12) shows a summary of some important values for your builds. Using this data, you can see whether you're close to releasing the build. Some of the information this report shows includes the following:

- *Active bugs*: How many active bugs existed at the time of the build.

- *Code churn*: The number of lines of code that have been added, removed, and changed in the check-ins before the build.

- *Code coverage*: Percentage of code covered by tests.

- *Inconclusive tests*: The number of tests that didn't succeed or were paused. If the build didn't succeed, the tests are either not counted or counted as inconclusive.

- *Failed tests*: How many tests failed during the build.

- *Passed tests*: How many tests were passed during the build.

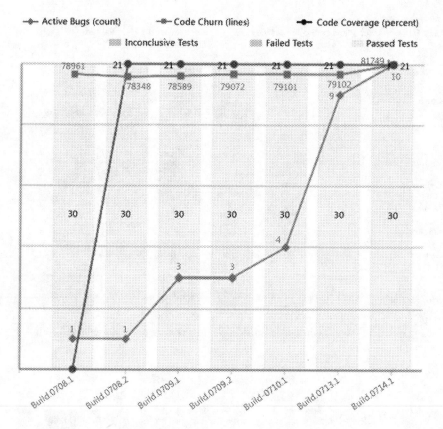

Figure 10-12. *Quality indicators report*

The *build success over time report* (see Figure 10-13) shows you the status of the last build for each build category (a combination of build definition, platform, and configuration) run each day. You can use this report to help you keep track of the quality of the code that you check in. Furthermore, for any day on which a build ran, you can view the build summary for that specific day.

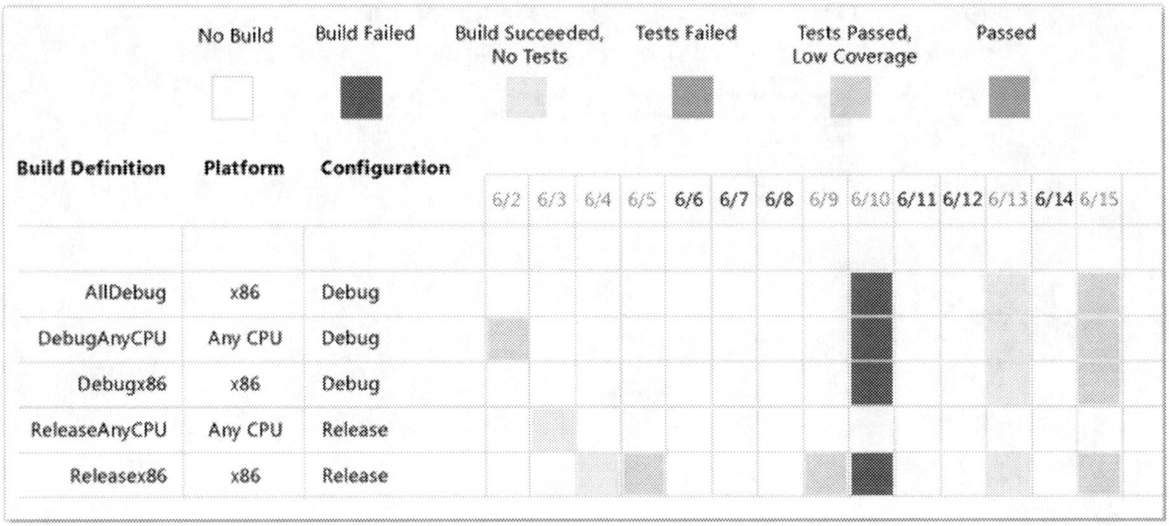

		No Build	Build Failed	Build Succeeded, No Tests		Tests Failed		Tests Passed, Low Coverage		Passed							

Build Definition	Platform	Configuration	6/2	6/3	6/4	6/5	6/6	6/7	6/8	6/9	6/10	6/11	6/12	6/13	6/14	6/15
AllDebug	x86	Debug									■				■	
DebugAnyCPU	Any CPU	Debug	■								■				■	
Debugx86	x86	Debug									■				■	
ReleaseAnyCPU	Any CPU	Release														
Releasex86	x86	Release			■					■	■		■		■	

***Figure 10-13.** Build success over time report*

The *build summary report* (see Figure 10-14) shows you information about test results, test coverage, and code churn, as well as quality notes for each build.

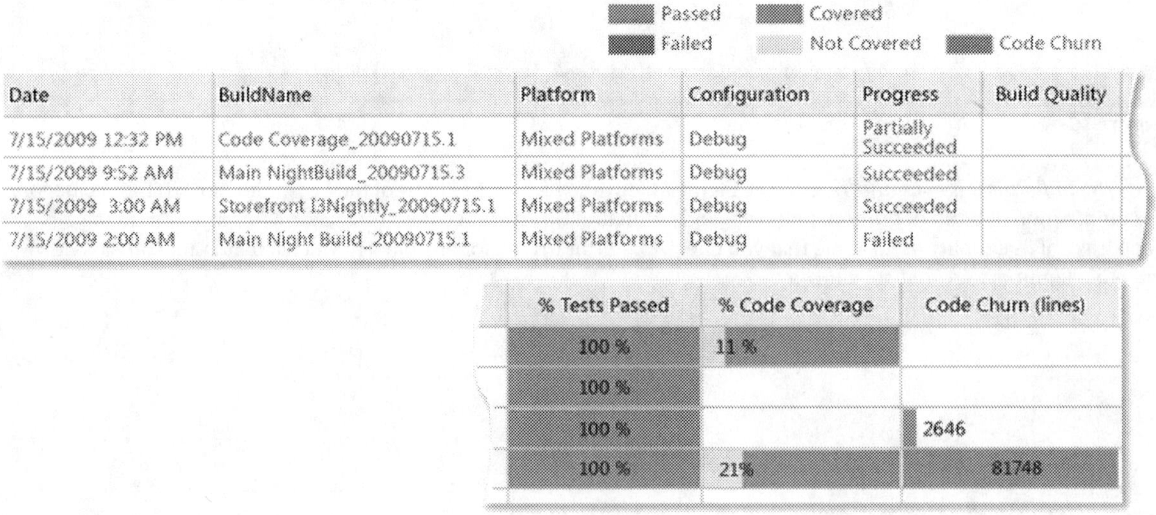

	■ Passed	■ Covered	
	■ Failed	■ Not Covered	■ Code Churn

Date	BuildName	Platform	Configuration	Progress	Build Quality
7/15/2009 12:32 PM	Code Coverage_20090715.1	Mixed Platforms	Debug	Partially Succeeded	
7/15/2009 9:52 AM	Main NightBuild_20090715.3	Mixed Platforms	Debug	Succeeded	
7/15/2009 3:00 AM	Storefront I3Nightly_20090715.1	Mixed Platforms	Debug	Succeeded	
7/15/2009 2:00 AM	Main Night Build_20090715.1	Mixed Platforms	Debug	Failed	

% Tests Passed	% Code Coverage	Code Churn (lines)
100 %	11 %	
100 %		
100 %		2646
100 %	21%	81748

***Figure 10-14.** Build summary report*

These metrics are suggestions that you can use as a base for following up on progress and quality in your projects. Different ALM tools offer different possibilities for reporting and collecting information. Thus it's important that you think through what you want for your organization when choosing an ALM platform.

Summary

Metrics and KPIs are valuable for any organization if you want to evaluate progress and quality. This chapter has shown some examples of metrics you can use for your ALM solutions. They can help you run your projects more efficiently and with higher application quality as an end result.

Keep in mind that different organizations find different metrics valuable. This chapter has given examples of metrics that are commonly used, but there may be others that are better suited for you.

The next chapter looks at ALM solutions from various vendors. We discuss their benefits and our concerns, to give you a better understanding of what the market offers.

CHAPTER 11

■ ■ ■

Introduction to ALM Platforms

Before looking at some of the most common ALM platforms, let's recap the cornerstones of ALM. As you saw in Chapter 2, a total of five important areas can help you improve your software development to deliver greater business value:

- *Traceability of relationships between artifacts*: There must be a way to trace requirements all the way to delivered code through architect models, design models, build scripts, unit tests, test cases, and so on, not only to make it easier to go back into the system when implementing bug fixes, but also to demonstrate that the system has delivered the things the business side of the organization wanted. Another reason for traceability is the need for internal as well as external compliance with rules and regulations. If you develop applications for the medical industry, for example, you need to comply with FDA regulations. You also need traceability when change requests come in so you know where you updated the system and in which version you performed the update.

- *Automation of high-level processes*: All organizations have processes for various things. For example, there are approval processes to control hand-offs between the analysis and design or build steps, or between deployment and testing. There are also project-management processes, continuous deployment processes, and more technical processes. Much of this is done manually in many projects, and ALM stresses the importance of automating these tasks for a more effective and less time-consuming process. Having an automated process also decreases the error rate compared to handling the process manually.

- *Visibility into the progress of development efforts*: Many managers and stakeholders have limited visibility into the progress of development projects. The visibility they have often comes from steering group meetings, during which the project manager reviews the current situation. Some would argue that this limitation is good; but if you want an effective process, you must ensure visibility. It's also important for team members to see how the project is progressing.

- *Work planning*: This includes planning functions such as defining tasks and allocating them to resources. Planning functions shouldn't replace the strategic planning functions that enterprise architecture and portfolio-management tools provide. Instead, they help you execute and provide feedback on those strategic plans. Integration with planning helps you follow up on your projects so you can get estimates and effort statistics, which are essential to all projects.

- *Collaboration*: An ALM tool needs to support the distributed development environment that many organizations have. The tools must help team members work effectively: sharing, collaborating, and interacting as if they were collocated. The tools should also do this without adding complexity to the work environment of your resources.

All these aspects are important in order to improve your development efforts. When considering a new ALM solution, keep these five pillars in mind and use them during your evaluation.

There is a tendency in today's market for ALM to be a little narrower and focus only on the development process. In our opinion, this is sad, because we think it's very important to take requirements management, portfolio management, and other nontechnical topics into account as well.

This chapter provides a short introduction to some of the top ALM vendors on the market. Keep in mind that the market changes constantly. Market leaders come and go, which may affect your decision along the way. One way to keep updated is to follow the magic quadrant from Gartner.[1] Gartner performs an annual survey of the ALM market and publishes an overview.

The following discussion is by no means extensive. It's here to give you a hint of what platforms currently are available.

Atlassian

Let's start by looking at Atlassian and its JIRA products. We have used some of these in various projects and can recommend them. We especially like their features for agile project management.

Many development teams use products from Atlassian in their development environment, but they're often closely integrated with open source products like Jenkins, Git, and others. This section focuses on the tools from Atlassian and doesn't go into open source tools.

JIRA consist of different modules so you can choose which parts you want. There are modules for the following:

- *Issues*: You can use JIRA to capture and organize your team's issues, prioritize them, and take action on what's important (see Figure 11-1). This allows you to stay up to date with what's going on around you. You get a backlog to organize and prioritize your issues as well as a Scrum board for your team(s) and also support for Kanban board.

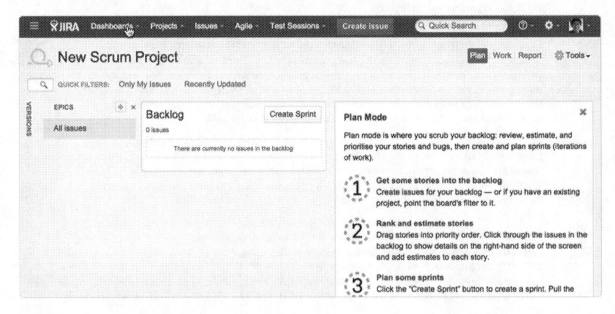

Figure 11-1. *Issues in Atlassian software*

---

[1]Thomas E. Murphy, Jim Duggan, and Nathan Wilson, "Magic Quadrant for Application Development Life Cycle Management," Gartner, November 19, 2013, www.gartner.com/technology/reprints.do?id=1-1N99LF3&ct=131120&st=sb.

- *Processes*: JIRA has workflows to match your existing processes (see Figure 11-2). You can adapt them as your team evolves or business processes change.

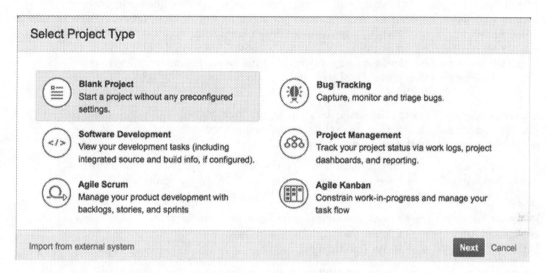

Figure 11-2. *Processes in Atlassian software*

- *Planning*: JIRA has tools to help you with agile planning. JIRA allows you to create and estimate user stories. You can build your backlog, follow your team's capacity and velocity, and get reports on the team's progress.

- *Collaboration*: Using the JIRA web-based interface, you can collaborate with your team and stakeholders. Atlassian has a collaboration platform called Confluence that gives teams one place to share, find, and collaborate on information they need in their day-to-day work.

- *Visibility*: To allow visibility into the team's progress, you can monitor various aspect of the development process and share this information using dashboards, wallboards, and more.

- *Version control*: Atlassian offers Stash, which is an on-premises source code management system for Git that's secure, fast, and enterprise grade.

As you can see from this short overview, there are modules to help you with most aspects of ALM. Table 11-1 provides some pros and cons for JIRA. Keep in mind that this list changes often, but as of the time of writing these are some of the things we see.

Table 11-1. *Pros and Cons of Atlassian Tools*

Pros	Cons
Flexible	Limited export and import functionality
Customizable	User interface could be improved
Good integration	Mobile support not quite there yet
Good third-party support	

IBM

IBM is one of the (if not *the*) largest ALM vendor today. IBM has a huge presence all over the world, and many organizations use its systems and applications. The IBM Rational Solution for Collaborative Lifecycle Management suite (CLM, which is IBM's version of ALM) has powerful tools to help you implement a good ALM solution. The IBM Rational tools might not be what the average project uses, but that's mainly because IBM focuses its solution on three specific domains: IT, including independent software vendors (ISVs) and system integrators (SIs); systems (complex and embedded); and enterprise modernization (host systems).

The suite consists of the following major tools:

- *Rational Team Concert*: Here you find the tools you need for running both agile and other projects. You can plan your work using work items, maintain source code, manage builds, and see general project status through various reports.

- *Rational DOORS (formerly Rational Requirements Composer)*: This application helps teams define, manage, and report on project requirements. It's a web-based application and has support for many project-management models like agile and Waterfall.

- *Rational Clear Case*: Clear Case is known by many developers around the world. It's a software configuration management solution that provides version control, workspace management, parallel development support, and build auditing.

- *Rational Quality Manager*: This is a powerful application that optimizes software quality across the lifecycle from requirements, to build, to test and defect management. Once logged in, the user is presented with a dashboard-based application where they can create new requirements, work items, test cases, and so on. It integrates with the other parts of Rational ALM as well.

- *Rational Software Architect Design Manager*: This tool helps teams collaborate and manage designs and design information. You can store, share, and manage designs and share with teams or team members across the globe. You can also use this tool to collaborate with stakeholders during design so you can make sure you capture requirements in the best possible time. All designs are stored in a central location but are accessible for all.

- *Rational Integrated Development Environments*: Here you find the development tools IBM offers. There are tools for web development, C/C++ development, Cobol development, and much more.

IBM offers additional tools that can help you in your ALM efforts, but these are the main ones. Table 11-2 shows some pros and cons.

Table 11-2. *Pros and Cons of IBM Tools*

Pros	Cons
Large customer base	Many applications need to be integrated to get a full ALM solution.
Supports DevOps	Some products seem to overlap.
Significant support for most aspects of ALM	Lacks some consistency in application GUIs, which can be confusing.
Supports both agile and traditional project management methods	High startup cost with a steep learning curve.

Microsoft

Microsoft has named its ALM solution Microsoft ALM. The heart of Microsoft ALM is called Team Foundation Server (TFS) and is an integrated package with tools for most parts of the ALM process. This is the ALM solution I have worked with the most over the years. This is available as a stand-alone product as well as a cloud-based version (just like software from Atlassian and others) called Visual Studio Online. According to Gartner, Microsoft was the market leader in 2013, closely followed by IBM.

TFS has a broad toolset of ALM features, and in our opinion not many other vendors today offer such a setup. As you can see in Figure 11-3, TFS offers functionality for the following:

- *Project management*: TFS has support for agile frameworks as well as more traditional project-management methods. These are stored in a process template that can be customized to fit your needs.

- *Requirements management*: This is one area in which we think Microsoft is less strong. Using work items like user stories, you can capture requirements as well as acceptance criteria. You can also create and share storyboards using Microsoft PowerPoint and use these as material for discussion with stakeholders and developers.

- *Version control*: You no longer need Visual SourceSafe anymore. TFS includes a good version control system that can either store data in TFS or use GIT.

- *Test-case management*: Visual Studio supports a lot of modern test practices like test-driven development (TDD), which is popular with agile teams. There is also a tool called Microsoft Test Manager (MTM) that a tester or test manager can use to create and organize tests in various ways.

- *Build automation*: You can use TFS to create a good continuous delivery process. In a modern application landscape, this is essential for development.

- *Reporting*: All data in TFS is stored in a SQL Server database. One benefit of this is that you can retrieve reports using Excel or SQL Server Reporting Services without having to look for that information in several systems. There is no support for other databases, however, so you're stuck with SQL Server.

- *Collaboration*: TFS creates a web portal for each project. This portal offers various dashboards and reports you can use to share project status information. You can also use it to let stakeholder create new work items (user stories, for example) as well as allow the product owner to see and prioritize the backlog.

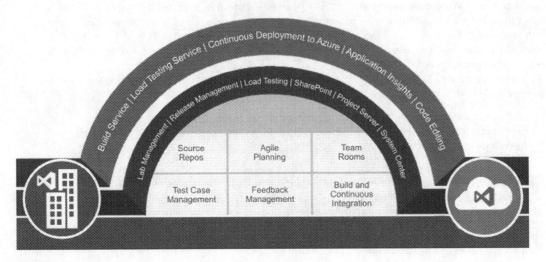

Figure 11-3. *Overview of Microsoft ALM*

Table 11-3 shows some of the pros and cons of the Microsoft ALM solution.

Table 11-3. *Pros and Cons of Microsoft ALM*

Pros	Cons
One repository for all data	Requirements management could be better
Significant support for most aspects of ALM	No licensing model for stakeholders or product owners
Easy to get started at a reasonable cost	
Extensible: offers an API you can use to write your own tools that integrate with TFS	
Support for Eclipse and other development platforms	

CollabNet

CollabNet's product TeamForge is an agile, open, extensible development platform aimed at distributed teams. By connecting teams, it helps organizations improve collaboration using a web-based system. Because it's so extensible, you can use all sorts of development platforms like Visual Studio and Eclipse on various platforms and integrate with TeamForge.

TeamForge provides a single integrated environment that supports planning, execution, software change and configuration management (SCCM), and collaboration. You can use TeamForge to automate your development process so that you can rapidly release applications. Table 11-4 shows you some of the pros and cons of CollabNet.

Table 11-4. *Pros and Cons of CollabNet ALM*

Pros	Cons
Great collaborative support for distributed agile teams	Relatively few products in the product line
Excellent integration with many development platforms	Doesn't cover all aspects of ALM
Significant open source support	
Good traceability in the development process	

We've presented a brief introduction to four major vendors, but the market is full of competitors that are also strong. The market changes, and the leader one month may be overtaken the next. Let's take a few moments to mention some of the strongest competitors as of this writing:

- *Hansoft* features solutions for ALM, Product Portfolio Management (PPM), and collaboration. The company supports both agile as well as traditional software development processes.

- *HP* has been in the market a long time. The company has primarily been a leader in software quality, but recently it has worked to extend itself into the rest of the ALM market.

- *Parasoft* offers a product called Parasoft Concerto. Its tools can help you with several ALM tasks including requirements management, project management, task management, quality management, and lab management.

- *Polarion Software* offers a single integrated ALM platform that supports highly collaborative team development with both agile and traditional approaches. However, the support for agile could be better—the lack of good Kanban and Scrum boards is a drawback. On the other hand, it offers great requirements-management support and has integration with both Eclipse and Visual Studio.

- *Rally* offers an agile ALM platform for distributed agile development. It's primarily a cloud-based ALM solution. Rally software integrates with most development tools on the market.

- *Serena Software* has a wide array of tools for both development and service management. It also offers tools to support both distributed and mainframe development. The product suite includes tools for requirements management, requirements definition (models, prototypes, and use cases), project management, quality management, defect management, build management, release management, task management, and source control.

- *VersionOne* offers an agile ALM solution that can help you in three important areas: centralizing planning, improving visibility, and simplifying collaboration. The software delivers tools that provide tightly integrated processes designed to guide and manage the entire software development value chain from idea to delivery.

Our advice is that you scan the market closely once you decide to improve your ALM process. You've probably invested a lot in your existing development environment. Keep in mind that many ALM products offer good integration with various developer tools, which makes the selection of a toolset a little less dependent on what you have in place.

Summary

This chapter has given you a brief overview of some ALM toolsets on the market as of this writing. If you want to know more about a specific vendor, most of them offer trial versions of their software so you can evaluate the products before you decide which way to go.

There are also some very good books that provide in-depth information on most of these tools. When it comes to Microsoft ALM, we suggest you look at these two:

- *Professional Application Lifecycle Management with Visual Studio 2013* (Wrox, 2014)

- *Pro Application Lifecycle Management with Visual Studio 2012, Second Edition* (Apress, 2012)

For Atlassian and JIRA, we suggest this book:

- *JIRA 5.2 Essentials* (Packt Publishing, 2013)

There are many factors involved when choosing an ALM platform. Don't blind yourself staring at the features of a specific product or solution—look at what your organization needs. Keep in mind that the tools shouldn't get in the way of producing quality software.

Index

Get the eBook for only $10!

> Now you can take the weightless companion with you anywhere, anytime. Your purchase of this book entitles you to 3 electronic versions for only $10.

This Apress title will prove so indispensible that you'll want to carry it with you everywhere, which is why we are offering the eBook in 3 formats for only $10 if you have already purchased the print book.

Convenient and fully searchable, the PDF version enables you to easily find and copy code—or perform examples by quickly toggling between instructions and applications. The MOBI format is ideal for your Kindle, while the ePUB can be utilized on a variety of mobile devices.

Go to www.apress.com/promo/tendollars to purchase your companion eBook.